Christlike

Christlike

by

Barry Applewhite

MOODY PRESS
CHICAGO

© 1984 by
THE MOODY BIBLE INSTITUTE
OF CHICAGO

All Scripture quotations in this book, except those noted otherwise, are from The Holy Bible, *New International Version,* © 1978 by New York International Bible Society, and are used by permission.

Library of Congress Cataloging in Publication Data

Applewhite, Barry.
  Christlike.

  1. Christian life—1960-   . 2. Jesus Christ—
Example. I. Title.
BV4501.2.A62   1984   248.4   83-24965
ISBN: 0-8024-0334-4

1 2 3 4 5 6 7 Printing GB Year 88 87 86 85 84

Printed in the United States of America

Dedicated to the directors of Pathfinders—
Kay Applewhite, James Killion, Charles Lamb,
John Milem, Sharon Pocock, and Frank Wichern
—and to the many people whose encouragement
and participation have made the Pathfinders
ministry a reality

Contents

1
A Blessing in Disguise

Bill Johnston sat in his lavish Portland office and marveled at how utterly unhappy he was. He had spent most of his adult life struggling and sacrificing to become a district manager, only to see his dream turn suddenly sour. His health was plunging, and his drinking had reached alarming levels. Bill did not realize at the time that this first-class crisis was actually a blessing in disguise.

Not until Bill hit rock bottom did he reevaluate his life and start finding the satisfaction his former life had long promised but never delivered. Curiously, what seemed like a crash allowed his life to soar to new heights.[1]

Matthew uses this same pattern—defeat transformed into victory—in his account of Christ's birth. He refers to the lives of two distinctly different believers to illustrate the pattern: Judah, one of Jacob's sons, and Joseph, the husband of Mary. Judah's behavior provides a black backdrop, against which the righteousness of Joseph shines more brightly. Both men faced extreme crises in which God transformed defeat into victory by bringing them to a higher level of spiritual maturity. Judah's crisis emerged from his own sinful behavior, while Joseph faced pressure simply by living in a sin-flawed world. For Joseph the crisis came with the birth of a son, Jesus.

[1]See Gail Sheehy, *Pathfinders* (New York: Morrow, 1981), chap. 4.

A CLUE TO MATTHEW'S THINKING

I'm probably not supposed to tell anyone this, but I find biblical genealogies boring. (I don't think even seminary students like genealogies!). Yet concealed within the Messiah's genealogy lies a vital clue to Matthew's literary structure for his story. I believe Matthew signaled his intentions by doing something quite strange; he included the names of five *women* in the royal line of Christ. To do that deviated from common practice; Luke mentioned only one woman, Mary, to make clear that Joseph had no biological role in Jesus' birth. Matthew named Tamar (1:3), Rahab (1:5), Ruth (1:5), Bathsheba (mentioned as "Uriah's wife" 1:6), and Mary (1:16).

If you read Matthew's first two chapters, you will quickly see that he wrote a very lean narrative. That is, he provided few details about the events he described. But Matthew cleverly brought additional material to bear in two ways: 1) by quoting from the Old Testament and 2) by drawing attention to Old Testament stories bearing intentional similarities to his own account. That's how the names of the five women have become important. Chart 1 shows how Matthew paralleled certain portions of his narrative with the stories of the five women in the Old Testament.

Chart 1	
The Literary Structure of Matthew 1-2	
Matthew	**Related Old Testament Story**
1:18-25	Tamar (Genesis 38)
2:1-12	Rahab (Joshua 2-6)
2:13-15	Ruth (Ruth)
2:16-18	Bathsheba (1 Samuel 12)
2:19-23	Miriam (Numbers 12-14)

In this chapter about Christ's birth we will follow Matthew's lead by considering the story of Tamar and her husband Judah from Genesis 38. Later chapters will develop the stories of the other women to supplement the story of our Lord's early months of life.

BROKEN PROMISES AND A CRISIS IN DISGUISE

In many respects the story of Judah and Tamar contrasts sharply with that of Joseph and Mary, because Judah and Tamar did not live as righteous people.

The story began when Judah left his family to go down to Canaanite country, where he found a wife who eventually bore him three sons. Tamar enters the story as the wife Judah obtained for his first-born son. But the son died so Tamar was promised to the second son. He soon died too, so Judah committed his third son in marriage to Tamar, although he really did not intend to go through with this pledge. (I'm sure you can understand that Judah considered Tamar bad luck.) Meanwhile, Tamar waited patiently in her father's house for Judah to fulfill his promise by allowing her to marry his third son. Tamar eventually realized that Judah had no intention of fulfilling his commitment. So she decided to take matters into her own hands.

After learning that Judah was going on a journey, Tamar launched a mission of her own to ambush the unsuspecting man. She waited by the roadside for him, disguised as a prostitute. Mistaking her as such, Judah struck a bargain with her. In pledge of a later payment, Judah left certain tokens guaranteeing the money. Those tokens were directly traceable to him. But before she could be paid, the mysterious woman (Tamar) disappeared.

In three months' time Judah heard the unsettling news that his daughter-in-law, Tamar, was pregnant. He angrily declared that Tamar should be burned to death. She, however, sent him a message that she was pregnant by the man who owned the tokens that she had sent. The symbols obviously belonged to Judah—she had conceived by his act.

This was Judah's crisis. To his great shame, his sin was exposed, and he had to relent of his intent to have Tamar executed. Judah had no further sexual relations with Tamar, and she gave birth to two sons. In a violent birth struggle one son stuck out his arm, on the verge of becoming the first-born, only to be pushed aside by his brother, who grabbed first place.

It's not a pretty story! The saga of Judah and Tamar reeks with struggle, intrigue, and sin. But amazingly enough, God used this reversal in Judah's life to shape him into a better person. When we meet Judah again in the Scriptures (Genesis 44), we find him offering his life in place of his brother's life—a much changed man.

I also find it striking that Matthew would intentionally refer to this story in relating Joseph's crisis, but I am convinced that he does. Both stories involve men facing crises that relate to the birth of the Messiah. In both accounts God turns defeat into eventual victory. Their crashes were blessings in disguise.

In chart 2, I have summarized a portion of the many parallels and contrasts between the two stories:

Chart 2	
Genesis 38	**Matthew 1:18-25**
A pledge to marry (11)	A pledge to marry (18)
A journey leads to conflict (12-26)	Same (see comments below)
Tamar taken to be a prostitute	Mary taken to be unfaithful (18)
Unmarried Tamar pregnant	Unmarried Mary pregnant (19)
Pregnancy revealed after 3 months (24)	Same (see comments below)
Judah calls for death penalty (24)	Joseph avoids death penalty (19)
Judah's plans reversed (25)	Joseph's plans reversed (20)
Judah declares Tamar's righteousness (26)	Joseph affirms Mary's righteousness (24)
No further sexual relations (26)	No further sexual relations (25)

THE UNWANTED CHILD—JESUS

> This is how the birth of Jesus Christ came about. His mother Mary was pledged to be married to Joseph, but before they came together, she was found to be with child through the Holy Spirit. Because Joseph her husband was a righteous man and did not want to expose her to public disgrace, he had in mind to divorce her quietly. (Matthew 1:18-19)

Clearly Joseph learned about Mary's pregnancy before hearing the facts of the matter from her. At this point, Matthew left much unsaid, but we can gain insight by considering Luke's account (Luke 1:26-56). God sent an angel to inform Mary of her impending pregnancy, and she quickly departed to visit her kinswoman Elizabeth in the hill country of Judah. She apparently did not inform Joseph about the trip.

Mary's story resembles Tamar's in several respects. First of all, her unannounced journey led to a conflict. She returned after three months of pregnancy to await her marriage in her father's house, in keeping with Jewish custom. Her pregnancy then became known, and the crisis hit Joseph full force.

Remember that Joseph had never read Matthew chapter 1! He had never heard any of the great hymns that tell of the Messiah's birth by his wife Mary. How would *you* have felt if you had been Joseph? He was a righteous young man of the house of David who had selected a godly young woman from among his people. After a three-month journey to Judah, his wife-to-be was pregnant. What would you have thought? Surely any of us would have drawn the same conclusion that Joseph did.

Joseph's many dreams of the life he would live with this woman he so deeply loved were instantly shattered. His life hit rock bottom, and he himself was probably subjected to scorn and ridicule because of Mary's condition. Certainly we must feel with Joseph the sorrow and pain of that defeated moment. Just as Judah mistook Tamar for a prostitute, so Joseph misjudged Mary as sexually unfaithful.

Joseph demonstrated a compassion that his counterpart Judah didn't show for Tamar; he tried to prevent any harm from coming to Mary. As an apparent adulteress, she could have received the death penalty, but Joseph took steps to quietly break the engagement. The Jews regarded infidelity during engagement as seriously as they did after marriage. On the surface we have another story filled with unrighteousness, tragedy, and defeat, but behind it all stands God, who transforms defeat into victory. He was using Mary and Joseph to accomplish a profound act in bringing salvation.

A BLESSING IN DISGUISE

> But after he had considered this, an angel of the Lord appeared to him in a dream and said, "Joseph, son of David, do not be afraid to take Mary home as your wife, because what is conceived in her is from the Holy Spirit. She will give birth to a son, and you are to give him the name Jesus, because he will save his people from their sins."
>
> All this took place to fulfill what the Lord had said through the prophet: "The virgin will be with child and will give birth to a son,

and they will call him Immanuel"—which means, "God with us."
(Matthew 1:20-23)

In the midst of disaster, God intervened decisively with Joseph and Mary. The angel urged Joseph to take Mary home as his wife and not to fear the consequences. That amounted to a legal, public claim of Mary as his wife, in spite of the fact that she was three months pregnant. The surrounding community doubtless misunderstood this action. Even though Joseph and Mary would have wanted to maintain a discreet silence, pregnancy cannot be physically hidden after a certain point. Stories about them were probably already circulating within Nazareth. The angel quieted Joseph's fears and revealed that Mary's child had been conceived by the miraculous, creative act of the Holy Spirit.

After predicting the birth of a son, the angel commanded Joseph to name the boy *Jesus*—a name filled with profound meaning. It is derived from the Hebrew name *Yeshua*, which means "the Lord saves." This name reveals the first part of what Jesus came to do; He came to deliver His people from their sins. Then Matthew tells us of another name Jesus was given, which revealed another part of His mission.

> All this took place to fulfill what the Lord had said through the prophet: "The virgin will be with child and will give birth to a son, and they will call him Immanuel"—which means, "God with us."
> (Matthew 1:22-23)

When we think of Jesus delivering us from our sins, we usually visualize it as happening *someday*. Certainly Jesus will save us from divine judgment on that day, but we fall far short of understanding if we don't realize that He came to deliver us from our sins *right now*. Immanuel, which means "God with us," brings home this present aspect. He continually transforms the defeats, struggles, and hardships of our lives into ultimate victory. Jesus is not the God-whom-we-will-see-someday or the God-way-off-there-somewhere, but, rather, *God-with-us-right-now*.

We may see ourselves as more like Judah than like Joseph, but that doesn't mean that Jesus will abandon us. His very name tells us He won't do that. Jesus Christ came into our world not only to resolve our sin problem, but also to transform our current defeats into ultimate victory.

A RESPONSE OF FAITH

> When Joseph woke up, he did what the angel of the Lord had commanded him and took Mary home as his wife. But he had no union with her until she gave birth to a son. And he gave him the name Jesus. (Matthew 1:24-25)

Joseph placed himself squarely within the camp of those who willingly respond to the Lord's revelation. He showed a willingness to take whatever risks would be involved in receiving Mary and her child into his home. By naming the boy, Joseph legally claimed Him as his own. Not biologically, but legally. Demonstrating his righteousness, Joseph followed the Lord's directives to the letter, trusting Him to turn this defeat into something good.

A BACKWARD GLANCE

In thinking back over these two contrasting stories, we find two very different pairs of people. God had to teach Judah and Tamar the very basics of right and wrong. Their story betrays no concern about what God wanted in their lives; their own self-concern was paramount. They sat in spiritual kindergarten learning basic lessons about life. Still God used them as part of the lineage of His royal Son.

On the other hand, Joseph and Mary certainly struggled, but their goal was to please God. Both were trying to serve Him in baffling circumstances. Through Joseph and Mary the Father brought about the apex of His salvation plan.

God's transforming power permeates both episodes and the lives of all involved. In both cases, defeat turned out to be a blessing in disguise.

LESSONS FOR OUR GENERATION

1. Perhaps this past year has been a year of pain, frustration, and defeat in your life, as it has in mine. I certainly do not want to deny the unpleasantness of such experiences. I wouldn't choose to have them, and I doubt you would, either. But when we become adopted members of God's family through faith in Jesus Christ, defeat takes on a promising new element. Our Lord wants to use our pain and misfortune to bring about strength, growth, and blessing. To accomplish that purpose He gets personally involved in our lives. To confirm this in Scrip-

ture, see Genesis 50:20; Romans 5:3-5; 8:28; and 1 Peter 2:10-20.
Use the following questions to evaluate your own life.

- Am I so absorbed with my adversity that I have lost sight of God's intention to bring blessing?
- What has the Lord taught me, or what does He want me to learn from my struggles?
- In what ways has God used misfortune in my life to change me and my outlook on myself and others?

Judah couldn't learn very much about his unrighteousness until he suffered a real crisis in his life. He wouldn't face up to his Canaanite associations, casual fornication, covenant-breaking, and vengeful anger until God brought him up short. In my own life I think I once felt a certain contempt for people who had personal problems. Inwardly I put the blame on them. But when I found out that what happened to them could also happen to *me*, it changed me profoundly. Such an experience allowed me to bring to others the comfort that God brought me in my crisis (see 2 Corinthians 1).

2. In spite of all their sin, the Lord used Judah and Tamar to help accomplish salvation for a lost world. Don't you feel a bit surprised that the Lord would use people like them as part of the royal line of Jesus Christ? But that's tremendous! It shows us that God can and will use believers of all maturity levels to bring about His purposes. The frailty and weakness of man does not hinder the sovereign power of God in cutting through obstacles to fulfill His promises. You may consider yourself a spiritual midget. You may be a person who has been running on the wrong side of the tracks for quite a while, like Judah. But the Lord can still use you. In light of that, can you personally affirm this statement?

- God will use *me* with all my flaws to help carry out His purpose for those around me.

But let's turn things around for a moment. In the story of Joseph and Mary, God clearly demonstrates His willingness to bring even greater blessings into the lives of men and women seeking to live uprightly before Him.

- Are you willing to make it your goal to move even closer to the Lord in the days to come?

A FINAL WORD

The last year has been the toughest one ever for me. I have even felt clinically depressed at times because of what was happening to me. As you can well imagine, I found it difficult to carry out my professional responsibilities under such a strain. But my defeat has proved to be a blessing in disguise. God has used it to bring about some basic changes in me that might never have happened without the stress. I have made some vital choices that will affect my life for years to come. Now I feel very good about myself and about my future.

My experience has taught me that Jesus really lives up to the name Immanuel, "God with us." Where He is involved, even a crisis bears the promise of eventual value.

2

When You Can't See the Bottom Line

Every generation has its own pet phrases to express things. When I was growing up, the word "cool" used to describe just about anything good. A little later on, things became "far-out." With the proper voice inflection and context, a person can make phrases like that mean anything he wants them to. Teenagers often coin such new expressions, but adults can get into the act, too. In conversations among men today, and especially businessmen, someone will usually mention "the bottom line" at appropriate points.

"The bottom line" probably derives its meaning from the world of accounting. When you get your bank statement, a little box on the page tells you the current balance. That's the bottom line. Most people looking at new cars will scan the bottom line on the sticker for a total price. And so this phrase comes to mean the outcome, the summary, or the end result of something. The trouble is that we can't usually know what the bottom line is going to be. What do we do then? In fact, we must decide some of the most important issues of our lives without knowing the bottom line. In choosing a marriage partner, a career, a home, and in many other cases we must make a choice without knowing the eventual outcome.

These uncertainties about personal decisions are compounded by other factors far beyond our personal control. Terrorism,

street crime, and economic crisis spread their fears into the
lives of almost every American. Faraway events can disrupt our
whole culture.

In such an atmosphere I find it comforting to know that
behind the scenes God rules as king over all. To know that my
allegiance to Jesus Christ makes me a part of His kingdom and
affords me His protective care helps to calm me in the midst of
many chilling threats.

HAUNTING SIMILARITIES AT JERICHO

As I suggested in chapter 1, Matthew intentionally hints at the
literary structure he is using in his first two chapters (see chart
1 in chapter 1). By using the name of Rahab, Matthew informs
us of a relationship between her story in the Old Testament and
the beginning section of his own second chapter. This key will
help to unlock the historical background for Matthew's story of
the visiting magi, who worship Jesus in the midst of a deadly
plot to kill Him.

In chart 3, I have outlined some of the similarities between
the story of Rahab and Matthew's account of the magi. You may
wish to refer back to this chart after learning more about Herod
and the events at the end of his reign.

Chart 3	
Matthew 2:1-12	**Joshua 2-6**
Magi seek facts (2:2)	Spies seek facts (2:1)
King and city disturbed (2:3)	Same (2:9)
Threat to rulership (2:3)	Same (2:9-12)
Search party sent out (2:8)	Same (2:7 and 22)
Magi succeed (2:11)	Spies succeed (2:23)
Return by another route (2:12)	Same (2:21-23)
King dies in Jericho (2:15)	Same (6:21)
Woman and family safe (2:14)	Same (6:25)

The parallel story of Rahab helps determine King Herod's whereabouts when the magi arrived. He was living in *Jericho* and not in Jerusalem. By correlating that fact with the history of Josephus we see that the magi appeared during the final few months of Herod's life and reign. Such timing fits perfectly with the findings of modern scholarship that Jesus was born just a few months before Herod's death.[1]

WHERE IS THE KING?

> After Jesus was born in Bethlehem in Judea during the time of King Herod, Magi from the east came to Jerusalem and asked, "Where is the one who has been born king of the Jews? We saw his star in the east and have come to worship him." (Matthew 2:1-2)

The Greek text of verse 1 provides a bit more dramatic impact than the translation given above. I would put it like this: "After Jesus was born in Bethlehem in Judea, during the time of King Herod, *behold* magi from the east *appeared* in Jerusalem." The magi suddenly and unexpectedly emerged upon the scene in Jerusalem. I believe they came secretly and quietly, similar to the way that the spies entered Jericho.

The magi asked a question filled with danger: "Where is the one who has been *born king* of the Jews?" Herod, ruling as a vassal king under the Romans, was not born of the house of David. Unlike Jesus', Herod's birth gave him no right to kingship over the Jews. The people hated him because he was not a Jew and also because he had killed members of his own family who were Jewish. And so the question posed by the magi meant double trouble for Herod. It reminded the people who heard it that Herod was not a Jew and that one had been *born* to be king over His own people.

The magi referred to the star of the new king and to their desire to pay this new king homage. Evidently the magi knew that they were coming to pay homage to a divine king.

A KING SEARCHES FOR THE KING

> When King Herod heard this he was disturbed, and all Jerusalem with him. (Matthew 2:3)

[1]Harold W. Hoehner, *Chronological Aspects of the Life of Christ* (Grand Rapids: Zondervan, 1976), 13-27.

To protect his throne, Herod had informers and agents spread throughout Israel. Herod ruled his country much like a modern communist country, using military force and any other means (such as torture) necessary to hold power. Herod was agitated by foreign visitors asking threatening questions about the throne.

I never had a problem understanding why Herod was disturbed, but it always puzzled me that all Jerusalem was alarmed as well. It all fell into place when I studied the period through the eyes of Josephus, a Jewish historian who lived in the first century. When Christ was born during the final months of Herod's life, the king was over seventy years of age. Herod had been stricken with various physical problems—literally from head to foot—and the Jews did not expect him to live much longer. False rumors of his death spread from time to time, producing confusion. In his final illness, Herod became even more ruthless and suspicious of everyone around him. Anything that threatened him increased the chance that people would be suddenly grabbed off the street, hauled off to one of his fortresses, and tortured for information.

The birth of Jesus brought a fresh threat to Herod's rule, but there had been others. In one way or another over the years, five of Herod's wives and seven of his sons figured into the struggle to succeed him. Herod dealt with his own family just as ruthlessly as he did with those outside. He murdered one of his wives and three of his sons over the course of his life, because he suspected plots against his throne. So for their own self-protection, the people of Jerusalem kept themselves aware of anything that might disturb King Herod. Such events could well initiate a new reign of terror.

Partly from Matthew's own hints and partly from the history of Josephus, we can confidently state that Herod was in Jericho when the magi arrived in Jerusalem. By living in his winter palace at Jericho, Herod could stay about ten degrees warmer during those months than he could in Jerusalem. And he also had access to warm water baths on the eastern shore of the Dead Sea. His physicians held out hope that those baths might cure his many ailments.

As Herod lay ill in Jericho, God unfolded His own movements right under the king's nose. Herod's informers arrived in Jericho to tell him of the magi and their search. But Herod could never lay a hand on Jesus. Part of the irony of the story involves the wicked King Herod's exerting all of his energy to find and kill Jesus, while the Lord casually brought His messengers into the capital city and on to pay homage to Jesus without Herod's ever being able to do a thing. Jesus and His parents enjoyed complete safety in the midst of grave danger because of the Lord's hidden rule.

> When he had called together all the people's chief priests and teachers of the law, he asked them where the Christ was to be born. "In Bethlehem in Judea," they replied, "for this is what the prophet has written: 'But you, Bethlehem, in the land of Judah are by no means least among the rulers of Judah; for out of you will come a ruler who will be the shepherd of my people Israel.' " (Matthew 2:4-6)

Herod summoned the religious leaders to his Jericho bedside, where he kept on pressing them for information about the birthplace of the Messiah. From the Scriptures they informed him accurately that the Messiah was to be born in Bethlehem. Even with this accurate word Herod could not alter the bottom line.

The material quoted from the Old Testament actually comes from two different places. The name *Bethlehem* comes from Micah 5:2, while the closing statement about Jesus being the "shepherd of my people Israel" comes from 1 Chronicles 11:1.

In both cases the immediately preceding verses have a message relevant to the passage in Matthew. Micah spoke of a walled city against which a siege is laid and in which a ruler dies (Micah 5:1)—quite reminiscent of the Jericho story.

Similarly, 1 Chronicles 10:14 tells how the Lord put Saul the murderous king to death and turned the kingdom over to David. Just as Saul often tried to kill David and prevent him from becoming king of Israel, so Herod tried to kill the son of David, Jesus. If Herod or his experts examined those passages, his threat level must have risen even higher.

> Then Herod called the Magi secretly and found out from them the exact time the star had appeared. He sent them to Bethlehem and said, "Go and make a careful search for the child. As soon as you find Him, report to me, so that I too may go and worship Him." (Matthew 2:7-8)

Herod summoned the magi secretly to his winter palace at Jericho. He took tremendous pains to extract precise information from them. Undoubtedly, Herod would have worshiped Jesus with the point of the knife if only he could. Herod hoped to turn the magi to his own purposes, but the mission that they actually carried out was that of the Heavenly King, not this earthly one.

HOMAGE TO THE KING

> After they had heard the king, they went on their way, and the star they had seen in the east went ahead of them until it stopped over the place where the child was. When they saw the star, they were overjoyed. On coming to the house, they saw the child with his mother Mary, and they bowed down and worshiped him. Then they opened their treasures and presented him with gifts of gold and of incense and myrrh. And having been warned in a dream not to go back to Herod, they returned to their country by another route. (Matthew 2:9-10)

The magi did not know that Bethlehem was their destination. They were relying on God's guidance to bring them to the right place. When the heavenly light appeared to them again, they experienced a joy verging on ecstasy.

The star that guided the magi was not a star in the usual sense of the word. This shining light guided them in such a specific way that it must have been a more earthbound supernatural light that guided them to their destination. Matthew tells us that the light "went ahead of them until it stopped over the place where the child was" (v. 9).

Conduct a simple experiment for yourself. Go out tonight, look into the heavens, pick out a star, and then ask yourself over whose home that star is standing. You will quickly realize that a normal star would not guide anyone to a specific location. Furthermore, such a star could as easily have guided the agents of Herod as it did those wise men. Efforts to relate this supernatural light to conjunctions of planets, comets, and other astronomical objects all amount to nothing but barking up the wrong tree. The star was a guiding miracle of God, given to a select group of men so that the Lord could carry out His plans in the midst of deep danger.

Jewish shepherds first bowed down to the newborn king, and

then Gentile wise men joined them in worship. I find it amusing that while Herod is called king many times in the course of this passage, no one bows down to him. Only Jesus receives homage and worship. Matthew was indirectly pointing out that Jesus was the real king, not Herod.

Just as the spies did not go back to Joshua's army by the same route, so the magi returned to their own country by another path. They avoided returning to Herod, and thus they completed the God-given mission undertaken with Herod's full knowledge. Under God's guiding hand, Herod proved powerless to stop them or to use them for his own purposes. God Himself wrote the bottom line.

HOW IT ALL FITS TOGETHER

Now we are ready to weave Matthew's account together with secular history in an attempt to reconstruct the events surrounding Jesus' birth.

As word spread that Herod's illness was incurable, his opponents in Jerusalem became more bold. Two men named Judas and Matthias incited a crowd to tear down the golden eagle Herod had erected on the Temple in violation of Jewish law. Suddenly, a rumor circulated that the king had died. Buoyed by this news, the crowd tore down the eagle. But the rumor proved false, and Herod's troops managed to seize forty of the men and take them before the king. In retaliation, Herod had several of the mob, including the leaders, burned to death. At about the same time, Mary gave birth to Jesus in Bethlehem, just five miles south of Jerusalem.

In his advance state of illness, Herod and his entourage departed for his winter palace in Jericho, from which he hoped to avail himself of the mineral baths near the Dead Sea. He was never to return to Jerusalem alive. After Herod's departure for Jericho, and some forty days after His own birth, Jesus would be dedicated by His parents at the Temple in Jerusalem.

With disturbing suddenness the magi had arrived in Jerusalem. They began quietly asking questions about the one who had been born king of the Jews. Herod's many agents soon carried word to him and greatly disturbed his suspicious mind. All Jerusalem feared the repercussions.

Because of his illness, Herod first summoned the religious leaders to his bedside to reveal to him the location where the

Messiah of the Jews would be born. Next he secretly summoned the magi to Jericho to reveal all they knew.

By this time, Herod's illness was growing worse, and the mineral baths were not helping. Expecting death, he became bitter at the idea of the nation rejoicing after his end. So he hatched a plan and summoned officials from all over Israel to gather in Jericho.

Meanwhile the magi, guided by a supernatural light, found Jesus and worshiped Him. Then they departed without returning to Herod. In response to a warning from the Lord, Mary, Joseph, and the child fled to Egypt. The timely warning spared them from Herod's own order that the children near Bethlehem be put to death. Herod became enraged when he learned that the magi had eluded him.

After ordering the death of Bethlehem's youngest children, Herod executed his own son Antipater, who was in prison in the winter palace at Jericho. Like the earlier rebels, Antipater had responded to a false rumor of his father's death, and it cost him his life.

Chart 4

Events Related to the Birth of Jesus

Golden eagle incident*

December	Jesus born in Bethlehem (Matthew 1:25)
Jan.—Feb. (?)	Sick Herod goes to Jericho*
40 days after His birth	Jesus dedicated at the Temple (Luke 2:22) Magi arrive (Matthew 2:1) Herod summons teachers (Matthew 2:4) Herod summons magi (Matthew 2:4)
Feb. (?)	Herod summons officials* Magi find Jesus (Matthew 2:11) Magi depart (Matthew 2:12) Mary and family flee (Matthew 2:14) Herod orders children killed (Matthew 2:16)
March—April	Herod executes son, orders officials' death*
March—April	Herod dies in Jericho*

*From Josephus, a first-century Jewish historian

Finally Herod instructed his family members to slaughter the Jewish officials that he had summoned to Jericho. He had put them inside an enclosure guarded by his troops. Herod hoped that the death of so many Jewish leaders would throw the nation into mourning instead of rejoicing when he himself died. But at long last, this ruthless, death-dealing man died in Jericho. Fortunately, the Jewish officials were not killed as Herod had wished.

A BACKWARD GLANCE

In the midst of an evil, corrupt kingdom, God sent a defenseless family and helpless baby to face many uncertainties and real dangers. But God protected them through it all and carried out His plan in spite of all opposition from others. That gives me tremendous hope as I consider the threats and dangers we face in our own world and our apparent helplessness. Through faith in Jesus Christ, we too belong to God's family, and He can write the bottom line.

APPLYING THE TRUTH TO LIFE

Use the following ideas to allow the principles from this story to change your own life:
1. God's sovereign rule over our world is a reality often hidden from our view by the clamor and tension of current world events. Too often we fearfully focus our attention on the news media and forget God. He has the power and authority to intervene at any level, including the personal circumstances of this world's most wicked rulers. I think these facts should lead you to take the following steps:
   • Pray for God's guidance of your own officials.
   • Pray that God will oppose the power of evil rulers.
   • Pray for the Lord's protective care over your own household.
2. Clearly, the obedience of the magi and Joseph to God's command spared them from death. Those who respond to the King of heaven and earth are shielded from much of the pain and sorrow that sin brings upon our world. How about you?
   • Do you see yourself as knowing God's revealed will, the Scriptures, so that you know how to respond to life-situations you face?

- Do you see yourself as one who generally obeys God's principles for living?
- Are you growing wiser and more responsive to God as each year fades into another?
3. What important situations are you facing right now whose outcome you can't see? How do you feel about the uncertainty? What involvement do you think God could have in your circumstances?

A FINAL WORD

I generally don't take risks unless I have to. So it still baffles me that before I went to Dallas Seminary I quit a secure job without knowing whether the school would accept me. To do otherwise would have delayed my application to seminary for two more years. It felt funny to burn my bridges behind me without having a clear path ahead. The bottom line lay far beyond my control.

In such times of uncertainty, God's hidden rule over my life helps to chase away my anxiety. I know that He can totally control the bottom line. Just as He protected Jesus and His parents from the evil schemes of Herod, so He can shield me in hidden but powerful ways. That knowledge helps me to take necessary risks and to make choices.

I hope that the assurance of His hidden rule will comfort you, even when you can't see the bottom line.

3

The Sword-Pierced Soul

I spent five years as an engineer under Admiral Hyman Rick-over, the "father of the nuclear navy." It made a profound mark on my life. His group gave me my first experience with work, and I often felt like I was chasing a fast freight down the tracks.

I'm sure that many things the Admiral said influenced me, but one particular comment has stuck with me through the years: "Wherever there is motion, there is bound to be friction." He used that engineering principle to describe the resistance and opposition that must be overcome in accomplishing change.

Rickover spoke of accomplishment in the face of opposition out of his own experience in fighting for a nuclear-powered navy. However, the same concept works in accomplishing things for God. Even when believers are moving in the right direction and living for Christ, friction will impede their progress. Joseph and Mary exemplified this principle in their long struggle to survive and to establish a home for themselves and their newborn son, Jesus. We can imagine no more godly endeavor than that, yet the friction proved intense. And it took a severe toll on Joseph and Mary.

God sometimes sets us in motion and then uses the resulting friction to shape us into people who can be even more useful to Him. He also allows opposition to challenge our willingness to follow Him. Those factors certainly worked on Joseph and Mary, as they struggled with external threats, their own fears, and apparently one another.

We too easily forget that Joseph and Mary were real people, just like us—a dad and mom who had hopes for their child and also a deep concern for their own lives. Through them God accomplished great change, but not without struggle against the friction involved. Yet the Lord proved faithful to them in their moment of need.

Because they endured friction in accomplishing change, Joseph and Mary give me great encouragement in my personal and professional life. For over three years I have involved myself in personal and group therapy to try to bring about constructive change in my life. I feel very good about progress in overcoming such common traits as perfectionism and a lack of deep friendships, but the struggle has been intense. I am sure that God has strengthened me, and yet He has not chosen to sweep all my obstacles aside. So I see the story of Joseph and Mary as having direct application in the lives of each of us as we strive to live for Christ.

MATTHEW'S LITERARY PLAN

In chart 1 (chapter 1) I highlighted the importance of five women's names in Matthew's literary plan for the first two chapters of his gospel. By quickly reviewing that chart, you will notice that the Old Testament stories of Ruth, Bathsheba, and Miriam underlie the part of Matthew's account that we will consider in this chapter. Matthew used those women as types of Mary and their experiences as illustrative of Mary and Joseph's experiences. He also selected Old Testament quotations to supplement his streamlined narrative. Thus, Matthew made some of his points by implication rather than by direct statement.

A FORGOTTEN PROPHECY

Christ's godly parents took Him to be dedicated in the Temple about forty days after His birth. During this trip many prophecies were uttered, most of them concerning Jesus. By concentrating on Him we can easily miss Simeon's specific prophecy to *Mary.* Simeon predicted the controversy that would swirl around Jesus and the way that His ministry would reveal the very hearts of men. He concluded by saying to Mary, "A sword will pierce your own soul too" (Luke 2:35).

The sword represents discrimination and division, rather than judgment. Concerning this passage, Raymond Brown says, "Indeed her special anguish as the sword of discrimination passes through her soul will consist in recognizing that the claims of Jesus' heavenly Father outrank any human attachments between Him and His mother . . . Mary here is part of Israel to be tested like the rest."[1] Little did Mary know how quickly the secret thoughts of her own heart would come out into the open in the events that would follow. She had been granted an unparalleled privilege, yet an unusual burden came with it.

DEATH HUNT

> When they had gone, an angel of the Lord appeared to Joseph in a dream. "Get up," he said, "take the child and his mother and escape to Egypt. Stay there until I tell you, for Herod is going to search for the child to kill him."
>
> So he got up, took the child and his mother during the night and left for Egypt, where he stayed until the death of Herod. And so was fulfilled what the Lord had said through the prophet: "Out of Egypt I called my son." (Matthew 2:13-15)

Using Matthew's hint as a starting point, I believe that the book of Ruth correlates with this brief paragraph. Ruth's story pictures God's protective care over His people. To describe all parallels between the two stories would take us too far afield. To inspire your own study I will mention that the book of Ruth tells about a *husbandless* woman who had a son (under righteous circumstances!). This son became famous in Israel and was part of the royal line of David. The story also involves a family that fled Bethlehem in time of great trouble to take refuge among the ancestral enemies of Israel. It suits Matthew's purpose perfectly to refer to this story of God's sovereign protection in troubled times.

The husbandless woman is Naomi (Ruth 4:16), who feels bitter because she thinks God has brought affliction upon her life. In view of the many parallels between the stories, I think Matthew subtly implied that Mary experienced similar feelings dur-

[1]Raymond E. Brown, *The Birth of the Messiah* (New York: Doubleday, 1979), 465.

ing the flight to Egypt. That may sound farfetched, but remember the prophecy concerning Mary, and consider the circumstances of the escape. Christ's parents didn't even have time to wait for dawn, but had to leave in darkness to escape Herod's troops. Many of us have never experienced mortal danger, so it's hard for us to grasp the emotional impact of such an experience. God's protection was quite real, but then, so was the danger!

Matthew's account informs us that the stay in Egypt led to the fulfillment of prophecy: "Out of Egypt I called my Son" (Hosea 11:1). Many scholars have commented that in this experience Jesus reenacted the national experience of Israel, except that He responded in complete obedience.

Fulfilling prophecy sounds great. However, after undergoing ridicule in Nazareth, traveling to Bethlehem in advanced pregnancy, fleeing from a death order, and leaving one's own country, we can certainly imagine that Mary went through a lot. She and Joseph had to take each step in an atmosphere of danger and uncertainty.

A REASON TO HOPE

> When Herod realized that he had been outwitted by the Magi, he was furious, and he gave orders to kill all the boys in Bethlehem and its vicinity who were two years old and under, in accordance with the time he had learned from the Magi. Then what was said through the prophet Jeremiah was fulfilled: "A voice is heard in Ramah, weeping and great mourning, Rachel weeping for her children and refusing to be comforted, because they are no more. (Matthew 2:16-18)

Matthew used the name of Bathsheba (Matthew 1:6) to connect his own account with the Old Testament material that relates to this section. We find Bathsheba in 2 Samuel, whose theme is that God establishes His king upon the throne in spite of sin and opposition in His path. This theme, God's overcoming royal opposition to accomplish His purpose for the nation, suits Matthew's account perfectly.

In Samuel, the king was tricked, became enraged, and as a result ordered death, a penalty that fell on the house of David. In each of these respects, the story in Samuel matches Matthew's story.

Realizing that he had been tricked, Herod flew into a rage

and ordered death for all of the children near Bethlehem under two years of age. The people called Bethlehem "the city of David," and this penalty fell on the house of David. Scholars estimate that about twenty young boys were slaughtered. Various opinions have been offered about why Herod killed children under *two years* of age. Some think this means that the magi had seen the star two years previous, while others simply see a ruthless man providing plenty of margin. For Herod to kill a few more people would hardly warrant special notice. He had done so before.

Matthew used the quotation from Jeremiah 31:15 for his own literary purposes. Actually, in the context of this Jeremiah quote, God *rebukes* Rachel. He then tells her, "They will return from the land of the enemy so there is hope for your future . . . Your children will return to their own land" (Jeremiah 31:16-17). Matthew was telling his readers that, in the midst of tragedy, God was working to bring hope for the future of His people in a child's return from the land of the enemy. In this way, Matthew continued to use a back-door approach to make comments on the events and characters involved.

I think that the rebuke of Rachel actually symbolizes a rebuke of *Mary* for her response to the terrible events of these days. That may sound like speculation, but I would remind you of the prophecy concerning a sword piercing Mary's heart and urge you to reserve judgment until you hear the story of Miriam, which underlies the final paragraph of Matthew's story.

MOTION AND FRICTION ON THE ROAD TO ISRAEL

> After Herod died, an angel of the Lord appeared in a dream to Joseph in Egypt and said, "Get up, take the child and his mother and go to the land of Israel, for those who were trying to take the child's life are dead."
>
> So he got up, took the child and his mother and went to the land of Israel. (Matthew 2:19-23)

Mary's name stands fifth and last among the five women Matthew listed in the genealogy of Jesus. We would expect this final section to deal with her life in a special way. Just as we trace the other women's stories through their Hebrew names, so we must look for Mary's counterpart in the Old Testament through her Hebrew name. "Mary" is derived from the Hebrew name *Miriam*, a famous woman in Israel's history. Matthew cleverly drew upon the story of Miriam from Numbers 12-14 to help reveal the deep struggle Mary and Joseph went through in returning to the land of Israel. They were in motion, accomplishing God's greatest act, and yet friction stalked them relentlessly.

The book of Numbers fit Matthew's literary purpose because it tells the story of the Israelites' struggles in returning to the land of promise. Miriam's opposition to Moses blends with the larger conflict of the people with God. Because of the Israelites' unbelief, rebellion, and disobedience, the journey that should have taken a few months took over forty years. The episode with Miriam retarded the march toward the land, and it could not resume until God had dealt with her directly and decisively.

I think Matthew was saying that the sword had pierced Mary's heart to this grave degree. God had to deal with her before the family of the Messiah could complete its journey back to the land of Israel. Chart 5 portrays some of the parallels between the Numbers incident and Matthew's story.

Chart 5	
NUMBERS 12-14	**MATTHEW 2:19-23**
Problem about Moses' wife (12:1)	Problem about Joseph's wife—see discussion
God speaks to Moses (12:2)	To Joseph (2:19-20)
Moses a humble man (12:3)	Joseph humble
Three called out (12:4)	Three called out (2:19-20)
God deals with Miriam (12:5-10)	God deals with Mary—see discussion
Journey continues (12:15)	Same (2:21)
Report about the land (13:26-33)	Same (2:22)
God directs new path (14:25)	Same (2 22)
Joshua set apart (14:30)	Jesus set apart (2:23)

A TALE OF DISPUTE AND CORRECTION

The problem between Miriam and Moses initially centered on Moses' wife, a Cushite woman whom Matthew would refer

to again later as he continued telling the story of Mary and
Joseph. Miriam then disputed that God spoke only through
Moses and claimed that He spoke through her as well. Moses, a
humble man, did not try to stop this rebellion, but left it in the
hands of the Lord. The Lord immediately called three people
out of the tent of meeting: Moses, Miriam, and Aaron. There
God revealed His anger against Miriam, in particular for her
rebellion against Moses, and inflicted her for seven days with
leprosy. After this brief delay, the people of God continued their
journey toward the land.

As part of the Israelites' preparations to enter the land of
promise, they sent spies on a reconnaissance mission. When the
spies returned, the majority spoke adversely about the land and
the prospects of conquering the Canaanites. This new obstacle
led to fresh unbelief among the people, so God directed them
away from their original destination. But along with Caleb, God
set Joshua apart as a man who had followed Him without reser-
vation.

HOW IT ALL FITS TOGETHER

Following Matthew's lead, I want to use the parallel Numbers
story to supplement what Matthew said about Mary and Joseph.
I suggest that Joseph was having a conflict with Mary, who was
rebelling against his authority to direct them back into the face
of danger—just as Moses had a conflict concerning his wife.
Perhaps Mary questioned whether God had really commanded
them to return, and stressed that the Lord hadn't told *her* anything about it. Joseph, a humble man like Moses, left the problem in the hands of the Lord. As a result, the Lord summoned
Mary, Joseph, and the child and dealt decisively with Mary's
resistance.

In the wake of this crisis between Mary and Joseph, the
journey continued until a bad report was received about the
land—like that from the twelve spies. The report concerned
Archelaus, the inept and ruthless successor to the dead Herod.
Archelaus had Herod's willingness to kill, but he lacked the
cleverness and diplomatic skill of his father. Because of this, he
quickly fell into conflict with the Jews and very early in his
reign killed three thousand of them in the Temple during Passover. I believe that was the report that was given to Mary and
Joseph, and it ignited their fears.

Matthew directly stated that Joseph feared to enter Judah and indirectly said that Mary struggled with the same thing (just like the Israelites). In response to this, God directed their path to a new destination, just as He had redirected the children of Israel when they struggled. Mary and Joseph would return to Nazareth, their hometown.

Even in this change of plans, Matthew saw a fulfillment of the words of the authors of the book of Judges: "He will be called a Nazarene" (Judges 13:5). To be a Nazarite means to be set apart to God from birth. Jesus, whose name is derived from the Old Testament name *Joshua,* was set apart unto the work His Father had given Him and to the fulfillment of all the promises of Israel. This resembles Joshua, whom God set apart to enter the land, defeat the enemies of God, and gain an inheritance.

ANOTHER GLIMPSE OF FRICTION

One final element of Matthew's account confirms the general interpretation of events that I have given above. The angel said to Joseph, "Those who were trying to take the child's life are dead" (Matthew 2:20). Scholars have long wondered why Matthew spoke in the plural ("Those"). They have also noted God's similar words to Moses: "all the men who wanted to kill you are dead" (Exodus 4:19). In checking out this reference I was amazed that it took me to another story (in addition to Numbers 12:1) concerning Moses and his Cushite wife, Zipporah.

In this puzzling episode, God called Moses and his family to return to Egypt and deliver his people, but that directive resulted in a grave conflict between Moses and his wife on the journey. Only God's intervention resolved the conflict and allowed the journey to continue. The similarity to the other stories is obvious; Matthew had clearly made another attempt to give the reader background information about the story of Mary and Joseph.

The story of Moses and Zipporah suggests that Moses did not do all that the Lord had instructed, and Matthew's use of this tale probably implies that Joseph failed in some of his responses, too. Matthew certainly informed us that Joseph feared to return to Judah, in spite of the protective hand of God.

A BACKWARD GLANCE

Supplementary information is wonderful, but I don't want it to distract you from the main point. In accomplishing God's

will and fulfilling their role in the salvation program, Mary and
Joseph moved forward only in the face of friction from every
quarter. Their experiences amply fulfilled Simeon's prophecy
that Mary would struggle within herself. Mary and Joseph were
real people—not the strain-free caricatures we so often carry
away from Christmas pageants. Their lives provide instruction
about the friction we too will face in bringing about God's
purposes in our own lives. He will protect us and care for us
and at the same time leave us under certain tensions, which He
also will use to shape our lives.

OUR MOTION AND OUR FRICTION

Use the following applicational ideas to bring this truth home
in your own experience. Remember that God teaches us His
principles to change our lives, and not just to make us smarter!
1. Discouragement, bitterness toward God, fear, and resistance
   to God's guidance all find expression at times in the lives of
   righteous men and women. We will never enjoy it when we
   see those responses in ourselves. Every believer will experience such feelings at points, though it takes emotional sensitivity and courage to admit to having those emotions. We
   cringe when we see ourselves resisting God.
   • We need to deal directly with such responses so that we are
     not impeded in living for Christ.
   • The Lord concerns Himself primarily with our overall atti-
     tude toward Him; He *knows* we will have lapses, and He
     deals with us patiently.
   God didn't dump Mary and Joseph because of their problems.
   He continued using them to play a vital role in the life of His
   Son. The Lord undoubtedly took into account that this righteous man and woman were facing tremendous pressures.
   He takes *our* circumstances and limitations into account as
   well.
2. Some types of personal growth take place only through repeated applications of pressure. I jog six days a week, but not
   because I like it. To me it's not fun. But I can't get into good
   physical condition without repeated applications of exercise.
   Some types of growth and change in life can only come
   through stressful experience. You can't learn everything you
   need to know out of a book. Even Jesus "learned obedience
   from what He suffered" (Hebrews 5:8). In spite of this reality,
   many of us think of learning as something that happens only

in a classroom. That's only the tip of the iceberg!

- What is Christ trying to teach you through your experiences—especially the hard ones?
- Focus particularly on repeated patterns in your behavior. Have you missed some important insights that could enrich your life?

Do you find yourself running into the same brick wall again and again? Do your failures tend to cluster in a certain area? What is God trying to teach you through those experiences?

3. God uses the hardships we face to prepare us for the future. I don't think He ever leaves us totally tension-free. If He leads us into a troubled situation, we can trust Him to be there with us. Ask yourself:

- What does the Lord want *me* to face?
- Am I facing it or running from it?

A FINAL WORD

During World War II, the Japanese sent kamikaze pilots on suicide flights in a desperate attempt to stave off defeat. Those men flew what amounted to bombs with wings on them. Most planes have *landing* gear, but Kamakaze planes had wheels that fell away on *take-off* so the pilot couldn't change his mind. Some of the pilots didn't appreciate the missions they were ordered to do. One man took off, flew his plane over his commanding officer's house, and strafed it with machine gun fire before heading out to sea. Such were his feelings! You see, those men were expendable in the eyes of their superiors.

God may send us into spiritual battle, but He doesn't consider us expendable. We are not like paper cups that God casually throws aside after each use. The Lord wants to use us, just as He did Joseph and Mary, but it won't always be easy, and our faith will be tested at times. As we live for Christ and grow in Him, we will accomplish motion only by facing friction. As He calls upon us to overcome great opposition, He will personally go with us every step of the way.

4
Final Exam

Some of my teachers are hard to remember, while others I will never forget. I never liked Mr. Crutchfield, but he won a sort of immortality in my hall of memories.

I made sure to get to his physics class early, and to sit down quietly. Almost two hundred of us would wait in the large, steeply sloped lecture hall for his grand entrance through the side door. His coming was an important event. You see, the moment Mr. Crutchfield entered, trailed dutifully by his grader, a holy silence had to dominate the entire room. Immediately! If some unthinking soul failed to see the mighty man enter, Mr. Crutchfield would look up with a scowl and snap, "Take out a sheet of paper." Then would come an all-too-regular pop quiz. At times, even when the room was just perfect, Mr. Crutchfield would give us a pop quiz anyway.

Fortunately, I will never have to face those surprise tests in physics again, but life throws its own little tests at me regularly. Although I don't like them any more than I ever did, I have to face them, just as you do.

Testing, trials, and temptations come in many forms. They swoop down frequently, if unpredictably, throughout the course of life. At such times, we must face the hardship of living in tension. Some tests strike with the suddenness of a thunderstorm. Other problems, such as chronic illness or an unhappy marriage, can linger for years with quiet savageness. That's bad news.

The good news is that Jesus thoroughly understands how it feels to take tests in life. He faced both kinds: the sudden, sharp tests and the long, grinding ones. Christ knows from experience what we so desperately need from Him in our hour of need. For Jesus every test took on the dark hues of a final exam, because His whole mission could have been destroyed through a single act of sin. By considering His model, we can learn how to endure when the sky begins to fall.

THE FIRST TEST

> Jesus, full of the Holy Spirit, returned from the Jordan and was led by the Spirit in the desert, where for forty days he was tempted by the devil. He ate nothing during those days, and at the end of them he was hungry.
> The devil said to him, "If you are the Son of God, tell this stone to become bread."
> Jesus answered, "It is written: 'Man does not live on bread alone.' " (Luke 4:1-4)

After being baptized to identify Himself with those turning to God, Jesus entered the wilderness to face the onslaught of Satan. To the Israelite mind the wilderness symbolized a place of testing. It also represented a place of purging and preparation for full possession of the Promised Land. Like the nation of Israel, Jesus faced trial in the desert, the scene of the nation's great failure under temptation. Jesus was the keystone of a new beginning for the people of God, so the Father tested Him to prove His qualifications for that mission. The Spirit led Him into the desert, demonstrating that this encounter for the Son had the direct approval of the Father. The Father had a totally constructive purpose for Christ in imposing this test.

The Holy Spirit did not commune alone with Jesus in the wilderness. An *unholy* spirit, Satan himself, met them there as well. He came to destroy Jesus and His ministry, if possible. If Jesus could be made to stumble even one time, then He would be disqualified as our sinless sacrifice upon the cross. At that crucial moment *both* God and Satan were operating in the wilderness. The two forces collided in the heart and life of Jesus Christ.

The Greek verbs make it clear that Jesus faced temptation

during the entire forty days. Luke draws our attention to the end of that time so that we can appreciate the tension at its greatest intensity. Jesus had eaten nothing, and by that time His hunger must have been severe. To hunger is not wrong, and to satisfy hunger would not normally be wrong, either. But to interrupt a God-intended hunger would be to defy the will of the Father.

In His hunger, Jesus was reenacting the experience of Israel during the exodus, but with one vast difference. The Israelites' hunger had led them to grumble against God in unbelief (Exodus 16), but Jesus never faltered in trusting the Father to meet His need at the proper time.

In meeting the test of the bread, Jesus quoted from the teaching of Moses (Deuteronomy 8:2-3). Moses told the Israelites that God had tested them in the desert to know their hearts. He had allowed them to hunger and then fed them with manna so they would realize that man doesn't live merely on bread, but by God's provision.

On the surface, it is obvious that Satan was tempting Jesus to end the God-intended test prematurely. But underneath that, I see this attack as an attempt to get Jesus to distrust the Father. In other words, I believe Satan was trying to disrupt the relationship between the Father and the Son.

Jesus could have met His own need easily, by converting the stones into bread as Satan suggested. But that would have demonstrated a lack of trust in His Father's loving care. Jesus passed this test with flying colors.

Our times of testing resemble His in some ways. Both God and Satan can simultaneously work in a given case. The test itself is often amoral, like a knife. A knife in the hands of a surgeon can cut out a cancerous growth and heal, yet in the hands of a murderer, the same knife brings death. So it is with testing. In the hands of the Lord it takes on a constructive purpose, but in Satan's it turns to our destruction. For this reason, the Greek verb *peirazo* can mean either "tempt" or "test." Satan *tempts* to bring destruction, but God *tests* to confirm obedience and promote maturity.

THE SECOND TEST

The devil led him up to a high place and showed him in an instant all the kingdoms of the world. And he said to him, "I will give you all their authority and splendor, for it has been given to me, and I can give it to anyone I want to. So if you worship me, it will all be yours."

Jesus answered, "It is written: 'Worship the Lord your God and serve him only.' " (Luke 4:5-8)

Matthew said that this temptation took place on a high mountain (Matthew 4:8). In the Bible, mountains often symbolize authority, power, or a kingdom. So in a symbolic sense, Jesus was taken to the very throne room of Satan, from which He could survey the entire kingdom that had fallen into Satan's hands. All the wealth, power, and glory of the earth lay within Christ's grasp in those moments.

With consummate salesmanship, Satan put great emphasis on the personal pronouns. "To *you* I will give all their authority and splendor, for to *me* it has been given" (v. 6, italics added). Satan brought all this pressure to bear "in an instant," perhaps hoping to bring about an impulsive response from Jesus. Jesus suddenly faced an opportunity to grasp something He should not have. That's an experience all of us have had and will have again.

Let's look more deeply at what Jesus was being asked to do. Satan was inviting Him to rule the world *immediately.* Would that have been wrong? After all, the world rightfully belongs to Christ, and one day He will return to rule over it. So it wasn't wrong for Him to want those kingdoms, but His time had not yet come. To have the world immediately would have meant the abandonment of His purpose to die on the cross for our sins. In effect, Satan was saying, "Jesus, instead of facing all the pain and discomfort that You will endure, why not take all into Your hands right now? It's so easy. All You have to do is bow down and worship me."

In that second test, Satan played the role of God by taking Jesus to that high mountain and showing Him the kingdoms of the world. Jesus saw what He would not *then* enjoy. This situation recalls the occasion when God took Moses to the top of a high mountain and allowed him to look at the Promised Land, which he would not be able to enter at that time (Deuteronomy 34).

The second test centered on immediate rule. On the surface, Jesus was invited to worship Satan. But to do that, He would have had to reject sole allegiance to the Father. Again, Satan was attempting to disrupt the relationship between the Father and the Son. Jesus maintained His sole allegiance to the Father in His answer to Satan: "Worship the Lord your God and serve Him only" (v. 8). Christ passed up unlimited pleasure and chose unlimited pain, in order to maintain His loyalty to the Father. Satan had been thwarted a second time.

THE THIRD TEST

> The devil led him to Jerusalem and had him stand on the highest point of the temple. "If you are the Son of God," he said, "throw yourself down from here. For it is written: 'He will command his angels concerning you to guard you carefully; they will lift you up in their hands, so that you will not strike your foot against a stone.' "
> Jesus answered, "It says: 'Do not put the Lord your God to the test.' " (Luke 4:9-12)

I agree with Alfred Edersheim,[1] who says that Jesus was taken to the highest point of the Temple at the time of morning worship. At that hour, a priest would blow a great horn, and the thousands of worshipers would pass through the great doors into the Temple.

The rabbis taught that when the Messiah appeared, He would do so on the roof of the Temple. They supported their dramatic prediction with several verses from the Old Testament. Knowing all that, Satan brought Jesus to a moment of great opportunity. Underneath Him walked thousands of those He came to save. As Jesus looked at the people, Satan reminded Him of a promise from the Psalms (Psalm 91:11-12). If Jesus really was the Messiah, then the Lord's angels would not let Him fall and die. Instead, they would save Him from harm. Such a miracle would undoubtedly have brought immediate acceptance of Jesus as the Messiah. By this tactic, Satan again tempted Jesus to avoid the cross and have the kingdom in an easier way.

In answering this enticement, Jesus again relied upon the Old Testament: "Do not put the Lord your God to the test" (Deuteronomy 6:16). Jesus stopped without mentioning the next few words of the quotation: "as you did at Massah." The sad story of Massah is told in Exodus 17. There the Israelites tested the Lord and said, "Is the Lord among us or not?" (Exodus 17:7). They

---

[1]Alfred Edersheim, *The Life and Times of Jesus the Messiah* (Grand Rapids: Eerdmans, 1972), 1:304.

insisted that God *prove* that He was among them by performing a miracle to provide them with water. They were wrong in trying to force God to act. The Lord doesn't have to prove Himself to anyone. For Jesus to throw Himself from that Temple roof would have been presumptuous and an insult to His Father. Jesus rightly rejected such a proposal. Again He triumphed where Israel had failed.

This third temptation consisted of immediate acceptance. Satan invited Jesus to force the Father to act in His behalf. It was another attempt on Satan's part to disrupt the relationship between the Father and the Son. The Son had come to carry out His mission in humble obedience to the Father. Unlike Israel, Jesus proved obedient, even under the severest pressures.

STRATEGIC WITHDRAWAL

> When the devil had finished all this tempting, he left him until an opportune time. (Luke 4:13)

Satan would come again. This had been an opportune time for him, but there would be others. Satan used people again and again to offer those very same temptations to Jesus. Consider, for example, the test of the bread. After Jesus fed the five thousand, they followed Him to the other side of the lake and tried to get Him to perform the same miracle again (John 6:25-30). He refused, on the grounds that they had only come to satisfy their physical hunger. They wanted to live on bread alone, rather than on the words that come from the mouth of God, so Jesus refused their request. He didn't come to be a magic man, and He refused to work that miracle because of the people's distorted spiritual priorities.

In the same time period, the test of immediate rule recurred. Because He had fed them, the people wanted to immediately make Jesus king by force (John 6:15). He rejected this alternative to the cross, as He had before.

Even as Jesus hung on the cross, the people taunted Him, as Satan had, by urging Him to prove His claims by saving Himself from crucifixion. They said that if He worked a miracle by saving Himself from death, they would believe in Him (Matthew 27:42). Thus the temptation of immediate acceptance was repeated. Jesus never accepted those temptations, in their original or altered forms.

THE TEMPTATIONS—A SNAP OR A STRAIN

Believers sometimes give the impression that such temptations were a snap for Jesus. They seem to think that Jesus felt no strain at all. But think carefully about the temptations He faced. He was asked to make a choice between limitless pleasure and unbounded pain. That's far more pressure than any of us will ever have to endure.

Christians often speak about the agony of the crucifixion, and certainly it was terrible. But Jesus experienced no more physical pain on the cross than thousands of others who had endured Roman execution. The *real* agony of the cross struck when the sinless Son of God became sin incarnate, by having all the sin of the ages dumped upon Him. Such shame and degradation surpasses our imagination. *That* was the unique pain of the cross. Satan invited Jesus to avoid such misery by simply bowing down and worshiping him. In this way, Jesus was put under pressure far greater than any of us will ever see.

When I am tempted, I sometimes give in. I suspect you do the same thing. In those cases, I never experience the full force of the temptation, because I cave in before reaching that point. But Jesus didn't have that luxury. He had to experience the full force and duration of every temptation that was ever thrown at Him. There was no easy way out for Him. In this respect, too, Christ's temptations far exceeded our own.

A third awesome element of Christ's temptations is that He had the worst possible opponent. I really don't believe that many of us, if *any*, are ever tempted by Satan himself. But Jesus was. Certainly we may face demonic harassment at some point, but Jesus was attacked personally by Satan—the worst possible enemy.

So if you ever find yourself thinking that temptations presented Jesus no problem, consider those three factors. In order to save us, Jesus had to forgo unlimited pleasure and endure unlimited pain. To be the sinless Son of God He had to endure the greatest force and the longest duration of temptation. And in Satan He had the worst possible enemy a person can have. In those respects, Christ's temptation far exceeds anything anyone else will ever have to face.

Use the following applicational ideas to take advantage of what Jesus teaches us in His resistance to temptation.

1. Satan takes delight in seeing Scripture distorted. This could even be done by isolating one verse and ignoring other pertinent parts of God's Word. That's exactly what Satan did in the third temptation. Every "Christian" cult uses distortion of Scripture to gain adherents. Use these principles to protect yourself from such practices.

- Gain a general grasp of the whole Bible; concentrate special attention on the New Testament. Even a general grasp can give you considerable protection, although the more you know, the better off you will be.

- Before drawing a conclusion from a single verse of Scripture, read the paragraphs before and after it. Is your understanding of the verse consistent with its meaning *in context?*

When verses are taken out of context, they are often given a meaning that God never intended. Even Christians with the best motives may inadvertently misuse the Scriptures in this way at times. I would suggest that whenever you read Christian literature and encounter Bible verses, you look each one up and study its context. Don't be lulled to sleep just because someone throws in a few biblical references.

- Avoid interpreting all statements made in the Bible to *others* as if they had been stated directly to you. Develop a sense for the difference between a general principle to be followed by all believers and a statement having only historical significance.

In many cases, we do this automatically. Let me illustrate by using two commands Jesus gave to His disciples in the upper room: "Love each other" (John 15:17), and "If you don't have a sword, sell your cloak and buy one" (Luke 22:36). Did Jesus mean for *you* to go out and buy a sword? (It *was* a command.) No, of course He didn't mean for you to do that. He was speaking about a specific historical situation.

But the other command, "love each other," is one that He wants every Christian to obey. How do we know the difference? Partly, it just takes intuition and good sense. A more objective method would be to consider whether another part of the New

Testament repeats the command. The apostles do not repeat the command about buying a sword in the rest of the New Testament, but we find the command to love each other restated frequently.

2. Consider the subtle way that temptation often comes. It strikes at our trust in the Father's concern for our needs. That's exactly what Satan did in the test of bread. He didn't come to Jesus to suggest that He go out and rob a bank, as believers sometimes seem to expect. No, Satan approaches in far more subtle ways than that. He leads us to question the Father's actions and to "cut corners," by letting the end justify the means; such was the case with the test of immediate rule. Or temptation may suggest that we take rash, willful action to end a time of testing; that was the test of immediate acceptance. And so we see that Satan will probably not try to get us involved in drug-running. Rather, he will try to get us involved in so-called "small" sins.

How about you? What are you doing to resist temptation?

- I'm trusting God to meet my needs.
- The presence of hardship in my life has not caused me to lose confidence in the Lord.
- I'm not going to solve my problems by taking the easy, disobedient way out.
- I'm committed to resisting rash or willful actions that I think would displease God.

3. Jesus understands and feels your struggles, and He helps those who seek Him. He was hated, rejected, unappreciated, attacked, tired, even moved to tears—just as we are at times. That's why the writer of Hebrews tells us that, because Jesus suffered when He was tempted, He is able to help us when we are being tempted (Hebrews 2:17-18). The same writer tells us that Jesus can "sympathize with our weaknesses," because He "has been tempted in every way, just as we are" (Hebrews 4:15). So, when you hurt, He hurts with you. He knows what you are going through.

Consider the following questions concerning yourself.

- Have you prayed for strength to cope with your test?
- Do you really believe that Jesus knows how it feels to live in constant tension?
- What problem or need should you take to Him today?

A FINAL WORD

In some ways our lives resemble a college course with its periodic tests. Assuming you are a believer in Jesus Christ, I have some good news and some bad news about your life course. First the bad news: You're going to keep on having pop tests. They will keep happening as long as you live.

Now for the good news: Jesus took the final exam in your place. And even though the course isn't over yet, your final grade has already been posted. You passed!

5

The Last Word

Just after a recent national election, I heard a defeated senator complain about the opposition of certain Christian groups to his candidacy. The senator accused those groups of violating Christ's own command: "Judge not, and you will not be judged."

I'm sure you've heard that argument before, and perhaps have used it yourself. Yet all of us make judgments about people in the common course of life. We do it almost unconsciously when we look for a "good" doctor or a "dependable" babysitter. In business, friendship, or marriage, people want someone they can trust; that means that some others cannot be trusted. Parents must often decide which of their children are telling the truth.

In all of those experiences, judgments are made about other people. In fact, I am making a judgment about you by saying that you do those things, even though I don't know you. I hope you won't conclude that I'm unfair, because if you do you'll be making a judgment about me! How do these common events stack up against Christ's command? The senator expressed the most popular caricature of what Jesus taught, but the senator was dead wrong. At least he pointed us in the right direction, because Jesus taught about this crucial subject in His Sermon on the Mount.

THE RIGHT WAY TO JUDGE OTHERS

> Be merciful, just as your Father is merciful. (Luke 6:36)

It was no accident that Jesus made that statement right before He gave His famous command about not judging. The statement shows that mercy is the backbone of all that Jesus said about judging. In order to understand what it means to "be merciful," consider the strongly related concept of compassion. Compassion involves being emotionally moved by another person's distress so that you have a desire to help him. It amounts to emotional concern for the other person, leading to help. Jesus was saying that, as we evaluate another person, we ought to do so in a spirit of concern for him. That means that we care about him, and that what happens to him happens to us. Jesus treated mercy as the leading idea and then dealt with judging others as a subordinate application of that theme.

JUDGING MERCIFULLY

> "Do not judge, and you will not be judged. Do not condemn, and you will not be condemned. Forgive, and you will be forgiven. Give, and it will be given to you. A good measure, pressed down, shaken together and running over, will be poured into your lap. For with the measure you use, it will be measured to you." (Luke 6:37-38)

Here we run smack into the main problem: What did Jesus mean when He said, "Do not judge"? That question can be readily solved, if we assume that Jesus knew we would need further elaboration and that He gave it immediately. In other words, when Jesus said, "Do not condemn," He was explaining what He meant by saying, "Do not judge." Believers are not to judge in the sense of condemning another person with harshness and finality.

I have two reasons for thinking that this is what Jesus meant. First of all, the cultural situation in which Jesus spoke supports this viewpoint. At that time, life in Israel was largely controlled and influenced by six thousand men known as Pharisees. They had influence far out of proportion to their small numbers. That's why Jesus could refer to them and say that a little leaven could leaven the whole lump. The Pharisees treated all others with extreme judgmentalism. They looked down on others with a scorn and contempt that would jolt us if we encountered it in our own culture. Their contemporaries considered them harsh, unfeeling, and severe in their criticism. People feared them, and not without reason!

To demonstrate the Pharisees' high and mighty view of themselves, I would like to recount a story out of rabbinic tradition. According to the story, on one occasion in heaven, God was having a discussion with the heavenly host about some difficult question of ceremonial purity. After tossing the question around for a while, God and the heavenly host couldn't resolve it. So He sent down to earth and brought up the leading Pharisaic rabbi to settle the question—as if the Pharisees could even teach God a few things! From that lofty vantage point, it isn't hard to judge other people!

Jesus knew that His disciples had been strongly affected by the precepts of Pharisaism. By contrast, Jesus used the Pharisees and their approach as a case in point of what *not* to do.

Here's my second reason for believing that Jesus meant "do not condemn" when He said "do not judge." Matthew records another occasion when Jesus was teaching His disciples the very same principles. Right afterward He gave them a command that made it obvious that they would not be able to avoid evaluating other people. He said, "Do not give *dogs* what is sacred: Do not throw your pearls to *pigs*" (Matthew 7:6, italics added). Jesus wasn't talking about house pets and barnyard animals; He was describing certain kinds of people. To follow this command, His disciples would have to be discerning and make value judgments about people, distinguishing the "dogs" from the "pigs." By using those terms, Jesus was referring to people who treated the Word of God and the miracles of His Son with contempt.

So Jesus was *not* saying that we can never evaluate other people or form opinions about them. He knew that His disciples would have to do that. That's simply part of life. But the spirit in which it is done makes a great difference.

Jesus next switched attention from the negative to the positive. He instructed His disciples about how to make such evaluations properly. Consider the literary arrangement of the four commands in verses 37-38. Jesus used an order that literary scholars would call *chiastic*, which means that the commands follow an "A-B-B-A" pattern. The "B" commands explain the "A" commands. And so in the case of the latter two commands, the thing that Jesus wants us to "give" is forgiveness. Here too the theme of mercy predominates.

The last part of verse 38 pictures the way in which God has generously given mercy and forgiveness to us. The picture comes from an ancient grain market. Suppose for a moment that you were going to such a market to buy wheat. After striking a bargain with you, the merchant would use his scoop to measure the quantity that you had agreed upon. If you happened to be dealing with a particularly generous merchant, he would measure the grain and then pack it down with his hand so as to make room for more. Then he would shake the container so that the particles would pack together more tightly. As a final step of generosity, he would allow the grain to literally run over the top of the scoop as he poured it into your outstretched cloak.

That's the way that God measures out His mercy and forgiveness of each of us. He doesn't miss a single opportunity to give us as much as possible.

BAD MODELS YIELD BAD COPIES

> He also told them this parable: "Can a blind man lead a blind man? Will they not both fall into a pit? A student is not above his teacher, but everyone who is fully trained will be like his teacher." (Luke 6:39-40)

This brief paragraph must be understood by using both culture and context. Jesus was warning His disciples about the deep danger of following the example of the Pharisees. He did so with a brief parable that not only asks questions, but also implies the answers—a wonderful feature of Greek grammar.

The first question anticipates the answer no. A blind man cannot lead a blind man. The second question expects the answer yes. If a blind man leads a blind man, then they will probably both fall into a pit. Jesus seemed to be asking questions, but actually He was making statements.

This parable reminds me of an embarrassing incident I experienced several years ago. The offices for our church staff were to be painted. One staff member kindly volunteered to get paint chips so that we could pick the color we wanted. Because I was buried with work, I simply told him to pick a color that he liked and use that for my office. Several days later, the painters arrived, and the first office began to get its treatment. The moment I saw the half-finished office it set my teeth on edge. My friend had picked a bright, *bright* yellow that reminded me of suddenly biting into a lemon. Then I found out that the man I had sent to pick out paint for my office was color-blind. I had sent a blind man to do my seeing for me.

But Jesus was speaking of spiritual blindness and specifically that of the Pharisees. He called them blind guides on numerous occasions. In effect, Jesus was telling His disciples that if they followed the harsh judgmentalism of the Pharisees, then they were no better than blind men following blind guides. They would soon meet disaster along that course.

Jesus challenged His disciples to consider carefully who they were going to pick as their model in this whole matter of judging others. If they were the disciples of the Pharisees, then they would become more and more harsh and condemning. However, if they considered themselves His disciples, then they must follow His lead in showing mercy. Over time they could expect to become more merciful.

LEARNING TO SEE

> "Why do you look at the speck of sawdust in your brother's eye and pay no attention to the plank in your own eye? How can you say to your brother, 'Brother, let me take the speck out of your eye,' when you yourself fail to see the plank in your own eye? You hypocrite, first take the plank out of your own eye, and then you will see clearly to remove the speck from your brother's eye." (Luke 6:41-42)

I wish we all could have been with Jesus to see the gleam in His eye when He used humor. These verses should at least hint to us that taking everything super-seriously is not a requirement for spirituality. Jesus pictured a ridiculous, exaggerated situation to drive His point home.

Imagine a man whose eyesight was so keen that he could pick out a small speck of sawdust in another person's eye, without even realizing that he had a telephone pole in his own eye. The word used for "plank" in verse 41 commonly referred to one of the structural beams that would hold up a building. The Pharisees could spot in others the tiniest infraction of rabbinic rules, while they utterly failed to realize how repugnant their own judgmentalism was to God Himself.

The key principle that Jesus expressed in these two verses is that whenever we evaluate others, we should always do it with one eye on ourselves. If we tend to see all of our problems as originating "out there" in the hearts of others, then we are basically looking at people the way the Pharisees did. Only by realizing that we have problems within ourselves can we temper our evaluation with a measure of mercy. Other people may differ from us in degree but not in kind. Every one of us has personal flaws and could stand some improvement. By dealing with our own motives and behavior, we can become better able to evaluate others with righteousness and truth tempered by mercy.

I do want to say strongly that Jesus is not suggesting that we must be perfect before we can ever get to the point of judging others. That meaning would produce contradiction not only with our Lord's own teaching, but also with other portions of the New Testament that instruct us about cases in which we must make evaluations and judgments about others.

I think we could summarize the whole passage with three principles. First, mercy must dominate any evaluation of other people. Second, it pleases God when we model our lives after people who evaluate others with mercy and forgiveness. Third, any evaluation we make of others should take into account our own share of the problem and our own flaws.

LEARNING TO SEE MORE CLEARLY

Use the following applicational concepts to help you in judging others.

Certain things in our own hearts can take us over that fine line into condemning others. Circle the items below that you think may lead you towards judgmentalism:
1. anger towards someone
2. personal weaknesses:
    (a) lack of love and compassion
    (b) an inflated or sagging self-esteem
    (c) a tendency toward perfectionism, dogmatism, and rigidity
3. learned response to certain kinds of people and situations

I know that I become more judgmental when I'm angry. If a husband and wife are mad at each other, they really know how to give it to each other with both barrels. The answer doesn't lie in either suppressing the anger or in allowing such times to degenerate into name-calling.

I think all of us know intuitively that some people find it difficult to express love or compassion toward others. For example, such emotional suppression has been deeply inbred in most American males. An interesting sidelight is that such people often find it impossible to love themselves. They become their own worst critics.

Regrettably, some groups of Christians simply exude judgmentalism. A person within such a group will quickly realize that he must either toe the line or suffer the consequences. How tragic it is for Christians to model themselves more after the Pharisees than after their merciful Lord.

Use the following ideas to help you evaluate others more accurately. Consider your own motives and purposes in evaluating others; if you don't really need to, then don't! Consider your own life; do you have credibility as an evaluator of the other person? Do you know them well and have their interests at heart? If you passed the motive and credibility tests, then use the following ideas to guide your evaluation.

1. Evaluate others from *alongside*, not from above.
2. Give others time to change and room to grow.
3. Be willing to revise your evaluations of others. Use other people's perspectives to refine your own.
4. Remember how it feels to be on the receiving end of judgment.

So that you don't misunderstand me, I want to say that there are some real "jerks" in this world. I'm not saying that there aren't or that that ought not to be your opinion of them. (Remember what Jesus said about "dogs" and "pigs.") I *am* saying that we must not reach such a strong evaluation lightly. I think we should also be quick to extend mercy if such a person shows signs of changing.

It may help to visualize two cliffs that you don't want to fall off of. One cliff consists of thinking that the problem always lies "out there" within other people, rather than "in here" within yourself. That view of life simply paints others as too evil and yourself as too good. But the other cliff can do you an equal amount of harm. It consists of an inability to show mercy *to yourself*. My own struggle with perfectionism has taught me a lot about how intolerant I am toward my mistakes. I act more like a Pharisee toward myself than I ever do toward others.

- Have you fallen off one of those two cliffs?
- Are you willing to try to change that area of your life with Christ's help?

Jesus warned that we must consider carefully who our models are in judging others.

I used to eat lunch regularly with a friend who spent most of our time together running down other people. I found myself constantly sliding down into the same pit. I had enough of a struggle in that area by myself. I didn't need his help!

Perhaps you should consider your own circle of social relationships, and also your church environment. Are those people helping you to learn more about showing mercy, or are they simply blind guides leading you toward the nearest hole?

A FINAL WORD

When I graduated from seminary, I knew the technical matters of theology, but I had a lot to learn about interpersonal relationships. I basked in the warmth of appreciation for my teaching. But a chill wind chased the warmth away when I first heard that I was not a "people person." That hurt. I responded by working hard to change myself into a more friendly person. And I have changed a lot over the years, but the chill wind still blows from time to time, and it still hurts. With a moment's thought, I'm sure you can recall similar experiences in your own life.

You and I are going to be evaluated by others for the rest of our lives. There's no avoiding it. The other side is that we ourselves will evaluate other people. Christ calls on us to use mercy in reaching such evaluations. We may speak the *latest* word about someone else, but Christ will speak the *last* word about them and about us!

6

The Number One Killer

Cancer. I'll bet that word ignites fear in you. No disease has captured the attention of Americans the way cancer has. I find that strange, because health statistics prove that heart disease kills far more Americans than cancer does. Yet when opinion surveys are taken in America, most people will invariably rank cancer as a greater killer than heart disease.

From these facts, I conclude that we are easily distracted by things that have a strong emotional component. Cancer seizes our attention and conjures up icky feelings of a lingering death. Other things that are dull and simple, even though vitally important, may easily be forced from our conscious minds.

In this age of media, we watch television programs with million dollar budgets on our color TV sets and become increasingly attuned to the flashy. One communications expert has said that our society has become so used to overstimulated communication that it takes sensory overkill to get people to pay attention.

THE LEADING SPIRITUAL KILLER

I'm happy to say that only a fraction of us will ever have to face cancer or heart disease. But I want to invite your attention to an insidious killer that threatens every one of us to one

57

extent or another. First, I want to warn you that this killer comes disguised in dullness and simplicity, so you are already conditioned to ignore it. I predict that some of you will feel little sense of urgency when I tell you what it is, and that's too bad.

This insidious killer is *spiritual heart disease,* a problem Jesus treated with utmost seriousness. In fact, He spoke about it in His very first parable. Jesus warned people from the outset that, if they wanted to understand anything else that He was going to say, then they had to deal with this problem.

In the early part of His ministry, Christ had gained wide acceptance and popularity. Because of His great miracles, people thronged from miles around to see Him. Once again the spectacular had captured men's minds. But Jesus had drawn some unfavorable attention as well, and agents from Jerusalem began to track Him around. Pharisees and Sadducees could always be found near Him, opposing what He said. They couldn't deny that Jesus had great power to work miracles, so they had come up with an explanation. They acknowledged His miraculous powers, but said that He drew them from Satan rather than from God. In response, Jesus rightly accused them of blasphemy against the Holy Spirit. As such opposition hardened against Him, Jesus spoke increasingly in parables.

THE FIELD AND THE FARMER

> While a large crowd was gathering and people were coming to Jesus from town after town, he told this parable: "A farmer went out to sow his seed. As he was scattering the seed, some fell along the path; it was trampled on, and the birds of the air ate it up. Some fell on rock, and when it came up, the plants withered because they had no moisture. Other seed fell among thorns, which grew up with it and choked the plants. Still other seed fell on good soil. It came up and yielded a crop, a hundred times more than was sown."
>
> When he said this, he called out, "He who has ears to hear, let him hear." (Luke 8:4-8)

Jesus had been traveling from town to town in Galilee in the manner of an itinerant rabbi. He was spreading the word about the kingdom of God and how men might enter it. Some who heard trusted in Christ; others flatly rejected Him; and still others had every response in between. The parable speaks of various ways that people respond to the Word of God.

Jesus said that some of the seed fell along the path, which seems like a strange place to be sowing seeds. But the farmers of Israel had clever ways of reducing the labor involved in planting a crop. They would take the family donkey and strap a sack of seed on his back. After cutting open the sack, the donkey would be released to wander at will around the property dropping seed. Some seed dribbled out onto the path. After the donkey had done his work, the farmer would simply go out and sow seed in the spots that the animal had missed.

The seed that fell on the path suffered a predictable fate—"it was trampled on." The Greek verb can mean that something is physically stepped on, but it also has the figurative meaning of treating something with contempt. We have the same idiom in English. Most of us have probably seen pictures of foreign nationals trampling on an American flag to show their disdain. This seed didn't stay on the soil for long; it had only a brief opportunity to take root. Soon it was taken away altogether.

The next portion of seed fell on rock. Many parts of Israel have thin layers of soil underlain by rock shelves. You can't tell the rock layer is there by looking at the soil, or even by looking at the plants. But as the plants grow larger, it soon becomes evident that their root systems have no access to moisture. After such a promising start, such plants soon wither under the burning sun.

The seed that falls among the thorn bushes also struggles to live. The thorn bushes compete with the new plants for both moisture and sunlight, thus making survival difficult.

Only the fourth type of soil, the "good soil," had any production, but what production! As we will see, this yield was God-given.

After telling this simple parable, Jesus did something quite extraordinary. He shouted in a loud voice to the crowd, saying, "He who has ears to hear, let him hear [indeed]" (v. 8). Jesus gave His words terrific emphasis in two ways: first, by the intensity of His shout, and second, by a grammatical construction that communicated an added impact to His listeners.

In the discussion above, I have introduced a small amount of interpretive material, but for a moment put yourself in the place of the original listeners. What would you have known, based upon the simple facts of the parable? Without interpretation being provided, I doubt if anyone would have known very much. In fact, I suspect that some who came out to hear the great teacher and miracle worker turned to one another and said, "Is that all there is? Is that all He's going to say? I didn't need to come out here to hear that!" I would suspect that some of Christ's listeners turned away and went home in disappointment.

> His disciples asked Him what this parable meant. He said, "The knowledge of the secrets of the kingdom of God has been given to you, but to others I speak in parables, so that, 'though seeing, they may not see; though hearing, they may not understand.' " (Luke 8:9-10)

The Greek grammar of verse 9 makes it clear that Jesus' disciples asked him *repeatedly* what the parable meant. That should lead us to question why they had to demonstrate such persistence. I think the simplest answer is that Jesus did not answer them the first time they asked. He didn't divulge the meaning of the parable to them immediately. He designed His response to act as a filter, screening out those who were resisting the teachings of the Word of God. But that approach also met the needs of those who had spiritual hunger, the receptivity of the human heart to spiritual things. So the ones who didn't want to know gave up and went away, while those heeding His command to "hear indeed" were granted deep understanding.

The Lord's method reminds me of what He said in the Sermon on the Mount, when He instructed the disciples to keep on asking, seeking, and knocking so that the door might be opened to them (Matthew 7:7-8). Jesus acknowledged His method by quoting the prophet Isaiah, who described a people who would see, and yet not see, who would hear and yet not hear.

> "This is the meaning of the parable: The seed is the word of God. Those along the path are the ones who hear, and then the devil comes and takes the word from their hearts, so that they cannot believe and be saved. Those on the rock are the ones who receive the word with joy when they hear it, but they have no root. They believe for a while, but in the time of testing they fall away. The seed that fell among thorns stands for those who hear, but as they go on their way they are choked by life's worries, riches and

pleasures, and they do not mature. But the seed on good soil stands for those with a noble and good heart, who hear the word, retain it, and by persevering produce a crop." (Luke 8:11-15)

In interpreting the parable, Jesus never revealed the identity of the farmer, but it seems obvious that He is the farmer. All commentators seem to agree on this.

Jesus interpreted the soils by describing four kinds of responses in the human heart to the Word of God. The first type of person proves *resistant* (v. 12); the second type is *opportunistic* (v. 13); the third gets *distracted* (v. 14); and the fourth is *receptive* (v. 15). Let's study each response in detail.

The first soil, that on the path, represents the resistant heart. I find that believers who study verse 12 often miss part of the meaning by jumping to the concluding part of the verse. Notice first that these people *do hear*. Even so, the things Jesus said do not find a reception in their hearts. Like the hard-packed ground of the path, the soil of their hearts don't take in the seed. As a result, the seed has no opportunity to penetrate. After a brief period, the devil removes any further opportunity "from their hearts." Here Jesus plainly identified the soil with the condition of the heart. He was talking about spiritual heart trouble and making a diagnosis. Such people have had ample opportunity, but they have failed to make any use of it, by hardening their hearts.

The second soil represents the opportunistic person. By "opportunistic" I mean one who lives in such a way as to seek short-term gains without any consideration of principles or long-term consequences. His approach says, "what's in it for me *right now?*" Jesus intentionally used the Greek middle voice for the words translated "receive" and "fall away." The middle voice frequently implies self-benefit. Such people either embrace the Word or cast it aside, depending upon whether it seems to benefit their purpose at the moment.

Christ made it quite clear that the beginning of hardship leads such a person to see no further benefit from the Word. That's when he falls away. It may be that some of the people whom Jesus was speaking about had been influenced by the Pharisees' charges that He worked His miracles through the power of Satan. Such criticism could have easily deflected the opportunistic heart from the Word of God. After all, such a person could expect expulsion from the synagogue for following Jesus as the Messiah. What benefit would that be?

A VERY MODERN DANGER

The seed that fell among the thorns represents the distracted heart. In my own spiritual heart this danger threatens me most. At times I allow the worries and concerns of this world to crowd out concern for what God is doing. When I ride in the car, I often listen to an all-news radio station that constantly feeds my fears about the economy, the arms race, street crime, and many other things. I'm not suggesting that I should totally isolate myself from those things, but I find that my heart is too often distracted by them. In most cases I can do absolutely nothing about the problem, and yet it occupies my conscious attention.

Jesus warned that distraction comes not only in a negative form, but in a positive one, too. The riches and pleasures of this world can also occupy the central focus of our lives. In many parts of the Western world we have an unprecedented chance to enjoy the pleasures and challenges of life. And we need not regard such opportunities as inherently wrong, because they aren't. But the pursuit of pleasures can achieve such dominance in our lives that it crowds out more important things. The dull and simple challenge of nurturing our own spiritual lives pales by comparison to the tinsel and glitter of our modern world. How tragic it is if we can only be reached by the sensory over-kill of our culture and not by the spiritual challenge of life with Christ.

I don't think I'm alone in this problem, because I live in a distracted generation. It concerns me that so many people in church hear God's Word and then walk out the door and soon sit down to watch two back-to-back professional football games. I love football, and I watch, too. However, the constant absorbing distractions that our culture offers do worry me. No one will keep this balance for us. Our spiritual heart condition is our personal responsibility.

Jesus says that the distracted person never matures. The stunted plant cannot produce mature fruit. That reminds me of Victor Belinko, a Russian pilot who defected to the West with a top secret fighter plane in 1974. Belinko told about how he became disenchanted with the Soviet system. As he flew his MIG-25 over the Russian countryside, he looked down on mile after mile of cornfields planted on Kremlin orders in unsuitable soil. It only grew to a one-foot height, and it never got any taller.

Belinko felt disgust; a lot of people had starved that winter in Russia. Failure to mature always has a high price.

A PICTURE OF HEALTH

The good soil represents the receptive heart that eventually has tremendous God-given bounty. Just as in the case of the other three kinds of people, the receptive person hears the Word of God. The difference is that he retains it. Actually, the Greek word gives the idea of holding onto something for all you're worth.

Several years ago I was standing on the deck of a submarine in the middle of the Pacific Ocean. A helicopter was hovering over me with a long cable and sling hanging down beneath it. They were going to use this rig to lift me from the submarine into the helicopter. Almost the instant I sat down in the sling, the young sailor told me, "Hold onto the cable." And up I went. You better believe I held onto that cable! There wasn't another thing on my mind. That's the kind of grip that a person with a good and noble heart gives to the truth of God.

But notice that Jesus said that retaining the Word is not enough; the fruitful person must also persevere before producing a crop. At this point we encounter another cultural stumbling block. I don't think Americans persevere very often. Yet a person can't plant the seeds and reap the crop the next day. Nor the next week. Nor the next month. It requires persevering care over an extended period of time before the harvest comes. Our cultural emphasis on the instant and the immediate strikes at the concept of perseverance.

I know many people who find it difficult to make commitments and stick to them. It's not simply because of difficulties that come along. Distraction often rears its ugly head and draws a person off toward some better offer. That concerns me, because the body of Christ requires commitment at every level. That's what it's all about—commitment to Christ and to one another.

THE WARNING

"No one lights a lamp and hides it in a jar or puts it under a bed. Instead, he puts it on a stand, so that those who come in can see the light. For there is nothing hidden that will not be disclosed, and nothing concealed that will not be known or brought out into the open. Therefore consider carefully how you listen. Whoever has will be given more; whoever does not have, even what he thinks he has will be taken from him." (Luke 8:16-18)

I hope it's obvious that most of the parable deals with the issue of salvation rather than Christian living. Jesus began by talking to an audience largely comprised of unbelievers. Their hope lay in allowing the Word of God to find a place in their own hearts so that they might trust in Jesus and have eternal life. Yet pertinent principles for Christian living can be drawn from each of the soils, or heart types. Certainly by the time Jesus spoke about persevering to produce a crop, He had gone beyond salvation.

The warning that begins in verse 16 was addressed to Jesus' disciples, who pressed Him earnestly so that they might "hear indeed." They had to take these matters seriously, because God always gives His blessings for a purpose. He has given the Word of God to instruct us, the Spirit of God to dwell within us, and the body of Christ to encourage us so that we can yield an abundant harvest. That's the meaning of verse 16. God has lighted the lamp so that it will cast light and accomplish His purpose. In this indirect way, Jesus challenged His disciples not to waste what God had implanted in their hearts.

Jesus also told them that in the course of time their response would become known. For there is nothing hidden that will not be disclosed in time. By application to us, that means that what we do with the Word of God will ultimately show up in our lives.

In His final challenge to His disciples to hear carefully, Jesus said, "Whoever has will be given more." That's the outcome I want in my life and in the lives of other believers.

TESTING AND HEALING OUR HEARTS

Use the following concepts to evaluate your own heart condition and your behavior.
1. In light of our Lord's parable, how would you evaluate your *general* heart condition—your response to Christ and His Word?
   • resistant
   • opportunistic

- distracted
- receptive

Would you rate yourself as opportunistic? The American mindset in the 1970s became so self-interested that it was labeled the "me generation." Self-interest can eat up everything else.

Or perhaps you are distracted. What will you do when there's Friday night football, Sunday morning football, Sunday night football, and more? Cable television may already make that possible in your area.

I know that I'm distracted. Not long ago a friend loaned me his electronic chess machine. He knows that I like chess, and he thought I would enjoy it. I took the chess machine and played it level after level to see how far I could beat it. I got up to the point at which the machine was taking thirty minutes to respond to each move. It would use that time to evaluate options before making its next move.

One night my wife and I were enjoying an evening with some friends. We were sitting in our living room. They noticed that about every half hour I would get up and leave the room. I was going back to my bedroom to see if the machine had made its move so that I could make my response. Suddenly it dawned on me that this machine was taking me away from my friends and causing me to do things that I would not normally do. Such technological gadgets excite us, but they can also be distractions.

2. The only way I can think of to determine whether we are receptive to God's Word is to evaluate our behavior. Do you think that God's principles are increasingly being integrated into your behavior as time goes on? What kind of feedback do you get from *others* about your commitment to Christ and growth in Him? I hope that they tell you that you are becoming more mature in Christ and that they see growth in your life. You probably won't get any feedback unless you overtly ask for it. Certainly I see value in each of us monitoring his own spiritual condition, but we tend to believe what we want to believe. Others may give more realistic evaluations.

A FINAL WORD

In every phase of life we must pay attention to priorities. I don't think I was ever struck so much by that fact as when I went to my first Dallas Cowboys football game. That was a long time ago, as you may realize when I tell you that the quarterback for the other team was Bobby Lane. My father had bought end zone seats, and we were watching the game through binoculars.

Pittsburgh had the ball, and their linemen came up to take position at the line of scrimmage. Bobby Lane, the old pro, was looking hard at the Dallas defense as he walked slowly toward the line to take the snap. The Dallas defense was jumping all around, trying to confuse him.

Distracted by the movements of the defense, Lane put his hands under the *right guard* to take the snap. Then he called the snap signal and the center (one person to his left!) snapped the ball straight up into the air. There was a wild struggle to catch the loose football when it came down.

The quarterback may know the defense perfectly, but if he doesn't get the snap from center, he's in big trouble! Bobby Lane had forgotten about priorities.

Our top priority is to deal with our spiritual heart condition. Only in that way can we yield a crop "a hundred times more than was sown."

7

Conflicting Signals

Anthony Brandt had a decision to make, and he knew it was a whopper. He was engaged to a woman who expected him to take a job with a steady, dependable income to allow them a normal life. He even had a job offer that filled the bill perfectly. But Anthony had dreams of his own that would take him along a more risky path. He wanted to fulfill a long-standing desire to write a book, but that path didn't offer the financial security that his prospective wife felt was so necessary. He was being pulled very strongly in two opposite directions.

Finally, Anthony made his choice. He declined the job and wrote the book. But in making his choice he paid a price; his engagement was broken.[1]

Anthony Brandt's decision illustrates the kind of choices we all face commonly. We live in a world that tugs and pulls us in many conflicting directions. As a result, we wind up saying yes to one thing and no to something else. Sometimes saying no can be tough because it involves rejecting something very good to do something better still. And that's hard.

In the midst of conflicting interests we must choose whom we are going to please. An old proverb says, "You can't please everyone." So who are you going to please? How can you make

[1]Anthony Brandt, "What It Means to Say No," *Psychology Today*, August 1981, 72.

such choices in a world of conflicting interests and demands?

I don't have any easy answers for living in such a complex world, but Jesus models an approach that will help us to sort out our choices.

JESUS MODELS A STRATEGY

To illustrate how Jesus handled this problem I have taken incidents from three different gospels. In each case Jesus faced a group of people that wanted something from Him. In the first story Jesus was pressure by His own brothers, who were trying to influence Him in an unfair and *coercive* way. Many people find it difficult to resist such family pressure. The second story involved a large group of needy people who wanted Jesus to meet their needs. They behaved in a *demanding* way. In the final story, Jesus interacted with His disciples. Like others, they wanted to take His life in a direction different from the one the Father had given to Him.

You see, Jesus had to face pressures and expectations just as you and I do. He was being pulled in many directions, and people were trying to make Him into different things. Jesus cut through those pressures and expectations in a remarkable way. The key to Christ's approach was to set His own life agenda by living to please the Father. That gave Him a very clear idea of what He should say no to and what He should say yes to. In other words, Jesus set His own priorities in response to outside influence.

FAMILY TUG OF WAR

> After this, Jesus went around in Galilee, purposely staying away from Judea because the Jews there were waiting to take his life. But when the Jewish Feast of Tabernacles was near, Jesus' brothers said to him, "You ought to leave here and go to Judea, so that your disciples may see the miracles you do. No one who wants to become a public figure acts in secret. Since you are doing these things, show yourself to the world." For even his own brothers did not believe in him.
>
> Therefore Jesus told them, "The right time for me has not yet come; for you any time is right. The world cannot hate you, but it hates me because I testify that what it does is evil. You go to the Feast, because the time for me has not yet come." Having said this, he stayed in Galilee. (John 7:1-9)

It turns out that Jesus was dealing with opponents here. I feel sad about that, because they were His own brothers. But how real that is! Some of the strongest pressures any of us face come from our own families. Our parents, spouses, children, brothers, and sisters wield enormous influence over all that we do. Family life frequently involves subtle tactics by one person to bring about action in the life of another. That's exactly what Jesus' brothers did in employing a manipulative technique.

From verse 1 we gather that the death plots against Jesus were common knowledge. Nevertheless, His brothers tried to set His priorities and dictate His actions to send Him into this danger, when they said, *"You ought* to leave here and go to Judea."* The translators properly supply the underlined words to capture the ploy Jesus' brothers were using on Him. They implied that He was not living as He *should.* (Pause for a moment here, and reflect on how many people try to tell you what you *ought* to, or *should,* do).

In their next stratagem, the brothers (wrongly) suggested that Jesus was seeking fame. By acting in secret He was foolishly squandering an opportunity to gain a following at the feast. I cannot personally accept the translation given by the *New International Version* in the latter half of verse 4, because John himself informed us that Christ's brothers did not believe in Him. The brothers actually said to Jesus, *"If indeed* you are doing these things, show yourself to the world" (John 7:4b). The brothers crassly dared Jesus to work His miracles where all could see. Imagine, an opportunity for Jesus to witness to His own brothers. What an awesome tug that would be!

One option Jesus had was to consent to their wishes and to try to maintain good relations with them. Or, He could have worked a miracle in their presence to try to bring them around. But Jesus didn't pursue peace at any price. He didn't put pleasing people at the top of His priority list. Instead, He said, "The right time for Me has not yet come; for you any time is right" (John 7:6). Jesus easily freed Himself from the expectations and pressures of His own family by a simple means; He made His own choices.

One lesson that emerges from this incident is that Jesus did not allow others—not even His own family—to set the agenda for His life. By application, this means that the Lord does not expect us to lead our lives to please other people. In fact, in following Him we may even suffer their rejection. Jesus also modeled a firmness in resisting manipulation. He did not automatically respond to the "oughts" and "shoulds" placed upon Him by others. Nor did He react to their scornful dares. Jesus showed us that living as a servant calls for courage and strength. Being a good Christian does not mean that we must comply with the wishes of others.

THE PRESSURE OF PEOPLE'S NEEDS

> At daybreak Jesus went out to a solitary place. The people were looking for him and when they came to where he was, they tried to keep him from leaving them. But he said, "I must preach the good news of the kingdom of God to the other towns also, because that is why I was sent." And he kept on preaching in the synagogues of Judea. (Luke 4:42-44)

This scene took place near Capernaum, a city on the Sea of Galilee. Jesus had moved there after being rejected by the people of Nazareth. When He arrived, He healed Simon Peter's mother-in-law from a serious fever. News of this miracle traveled quickly through the city, and before long the whole town had gathered (Mark 1:32-34). Jesus stayed up late into the night, meeting people's needs.

We join Luke's story on the following morning, well before dawn, when Jesus had gone out into the countryside to pray alone. Jesus was acting according to a spiritual priority, that of prayer to His Father. That was more important to Him than what other people wanted.

Although Jesus had met many needs among people in the city of Capernaum on the previous night, undoubtedly many needs remained. The people from the city searched diligently for Him. The English translation fails to make clear that those people actually tried to restrain Christ from leaving. They physically tried to hinder His departure. They didn't want to let go of this miracle worker who had done such great things for their town.

If Capernaum could have a man like that around for a few years, just think how good it would be for the community, they must have thought. Jesus would have become a civic treasure that they could have shown off to their profit and glory.

Jesus realized that their motivation was not a response to God's claims upon them, but a desire to experience more miracles. Would it have been evil for Jesus to stay in Capernaum to work more miracles? Would it have been wrong for Him to continue preaching the gospel there? No! That would have been a very good thing, but sometimes the good can be the enemy of the best. Those people had legitimate needs, in spite of their poor motivation.

But Jesus didn't respond automatically every time He encountered a human need; He had to decide whether to meet such needs or not. He weighed their needs against what His Father had sent Him to do. And for Him to stay and become the great miracle worker of Capernaum would have been inconsistent with what the Father had purposed. Jesus didn't come to be the great doctor of Galilee or the favorite son of Capernaum. He came to be the Savior of the world. Because Jesus had a clear idea of His own priorities, He was able to say yes to some things. To other things, even to good things, He said no.

Jesus told the crowd that He "must" leave them to preach elsewhere, in keeping with His mission. Undoubtedly that announcement led to disappointment, frustration, and anger on the part of those who so desperately wanted Him to stay. Even to us it may seem that Christ didn't take advantage of a great evangelistic opportunity. Here He had a crowd that was ready to eat out of His hand, and yet He moved on. It's jolting to see how differently He operated than we do. He turned His back on the needy people of Capernaum and went on to accomplish His mission without regret or apology.

We, too, will encounter demanding people in the course of our lives. Some of them will be believers and may need us to be involved in good and godly causes. Others will be unbelievers who desperately need to know the Lord Jesus Christ. But just because these people have needs doesn't necessarily mean that we are the ones to meet them. I realize that we could use such thinking to cop out on some legitimate responsibilities before God. But it concerns me that Christians can easily let the pressing needs of people set the whole agenda of their lives, instead of making their own choices with guidance from the Lord.

SHATTERED EXPECTATIONS

Very early in the morning, while it was still dark, Jesus got up, left the house and went off to a solitary place, where he prayed.

> Simon and his companions went to look for him, and when they
> found him, they exclaimed: "Everyone is looking for you!"
>   Jesus replied, "Let us go somewhere else—to the nearby vil-
> lages—so I can preach there also. That is why I have come." So he
> traveled throughout Galilee, preaching in their synagogues and
> driving out demons. (Mark 1:35-39)

Mark here described exactly the same incident that we previously looked at in the gospel of Luke. But Mark's perspective
was different. Luke focused his attention on the interaction
between Jesus and the seeking multitudes. Mark concentrated
on the relationship between Jesus and the disciples during the
same set of events. We would probably assume that Christ's
disciples would have responded in a more mature and understanding manner toward Him in this situation. We naturally
have a higher level of expectations about the disciples. (So
much the worse for our expectations!)

As Simon and the others looked for Jesus, they searched with
a special kind of intensity, as expressed by the Greek verb. The
verb is also used of hunting for an animal or hunting for a
fugitive from justice. They seemed driven by a special intensity
to find Him, and we soon discover the source of that intensity.
They said, "Everyone is looking for you!" This statement has an
air of rebuke and displeasure in it. It is as if the disciples were
saying, "Jesus, what are You doing out here? Capernaum is
where You're needed. And the people are getting upset with *us*,
because we don't know where You are. You're not where we
expected You to be." So Jesus had to deal with the expectations
of His disciples, especially Simon, because Capernaum was his
hometown. The disciples wanted Jesus to go right back into
town and do His thing. Even as their Lord and leader, Jesus
must have cared about what His disciples thought of Him, and
with the multitudes also searching and perhaps not far behind,
they wanted Him to go back and meet those needs.

But in His remarkable way, Jesus did not bend to the expectations of His disciples. He didn't say yes based on what people
expected out of Him. As the multitudes sought Him and the
disciples exhorted Him, He said, "Let us go somewhere
else . . . so I can preach there also. That is why I have come."
The reason we find this startling is because our expectations
tend to be like those of the disciples. But Jesus made His own
decisions based on His own priorities.

Jesus did not necessarily respond to people's expectations, even those coming from people who were very important to Him. In the three passages we have examined, people tried to use manipulation, demands, needs, and expectations to compel our Lord to take certain actions. He simply didn't let that happen.

In the face of the many attempts of others to impress their wills upon Him, Jesus maintained autonomy, the freedom to make His own choices before God. His example sets me free, because I have led most of my life giving in to the manipulations, demands, needs, and expectations of others. I'm sure that I acted that way for many reasons, and partly because I thought it was the moral, or right, way to act. But Jesus' example forces me to reexamine the whole question and to see that if I am to be a responsible person before God, then I must sometimes say no to others.

THE COMPASSIONATE CHRIST

> A man with leprosy came to him and begged him on his knees, "If you are willing, you can make me clean."
> Filled with compassion, Jesus reached out his hand and touched the man. "I am willing," he said. "Be clean!" Immediately the leprosy left him and he was cured. (Mark 1:40-42)

As Jesus walked away from the demanding multitude, He encountered a man with leprosy, who begged Him for mercy. I am confident that Mark included this story to show that Jesus didn't make His choices in an uncaring way. He deeply cared about the pain of this man, as He did about the pain of others. He met his need and cleansed him of leprosy. Jesus lived compassionately, but He was not about to be diverted from His primary mission in order to become something else. He came primarily to be the Savior, not the healer.

No wonder our Lord's sensitive heart was filled with compassion. Leprosy savagely attacks the body and often leads to the ugly loss of fingers, toes, and other bodily parts. Perhaps worse than that, lepers in Israel had to walk about shouting, "Unclean! Unclean!" Imagine how you would have felt, calling attention to your own ravaged body in that way. But our caring Savior had a cry of His own: "Be clean!" Even beyond that, Jesus *touched* the man—something no Pharisee would ever do. Jesus touched the untouchable because that's the kind of person He was.

In summary, Mark presented this careful balance: *Jesus cared deeply about people's needs, but His life was not ruled by them.*

FINDING YOUR OWN WAY THROUGH THE MAZE

Our lives confront us with a bewildering array of tactics, demands, needs, and expectations. Use the following application concepts to try to clarify your own life in these areas.

1. Here are several questions to help you define the main sources of pressure, expectations, and demands in your life.

- Who primarily influences your life agenda (i.e., how you spend your time and what you're trying to do)? Is it your parents, your boss, your mate? Who really dictates how your life is lived?

Whoever you name may be robbing you of your responsibility before God to make choices about your own life.

- Who in your life places significant expectations on you?

Jesus' disciples certainly had expectations for Him. They wanted Him to go back down to Capernaum to heal more people. Are there people in your life like that? It's not evil for them to have such expectations, but should you meet them? Should you affirm them, or say no?

- Whose rejection, criticism, or disapproval most influences your choices and behavior?

Do you think Jesus wanted to be rejected by His brothers? Of course not! Do you think He wanted to fail to meet the expectations of His disciples? He knew that would cause some friction.

There are people whose rejection wouldn't phase me at all. And yet certain other people's disapproval can devastate me. My life tends to be wrapped up in trying to please the latter group of people. In fact, I can get so wrapped up in pleasing them that I even lose sight of pleasing God. Is it the same for you?

- Who in your life tends to use guilt, withdrawal of love, or threats to get certain responses from you?

Some people directly or indirectly say to us, "If you really love me, you will do—" That falls in the same category as the kind of thing Jesus' brothers were attempting to pull on Him.

2. You determine who you are by what you affirm and what you

refuse. Saying yes and no are two of the most important tools you have in living your life for Christ. Many of us have good intentions, but what we actually do with our lives says a lot more about who we really are.

If saying yes and no are so important, then a deep problem exists. Very few people know how to say no. Some experiments were conducted at Yale in the 1960s to test people's ability to say no. The subjects in one room were told that the group in the next room had a set of questions to answer. If the people in the second room answered incorrectly, the people in the first room were supposed to push a button to give them an electric shock, punishing them for making a wrong answer.

As time went on, the people in the first room were told that the shocks they were giving had increased to the point that the unseen people next door were actually screaming in pain, or even dead. Yet when they were commanded to push the button and shock the people next door, most were unable to say no, so they continued the (imaginary) shocks.[2] We may wish that most subjects had said, "Wait a minute! This is hurting people, and I'm not going to do it!" But most of them found it too hard to say no.

- If Jesus Christ restructured your life today, where would He say yes, and where would He say no?

3. To say yes and no effectively, we need guidance from God more than anything else. Our family, our friends, and our culture can play constructive parts in setting our course, but they cannot replace wisdom from God. I'm not talking about believers' trying to ferret out the "hidden will of God." Instead, I mean that we need to have the principles of God's Word at our disposal to guide the choices that we make as we live our lives for Christ. God's will stands revealed in His Word. To help you gain this wisdom, I would encourage you to set three goals:

(1) To spend time reading God's Word
(2) To spend time in prayer
(3) To spend time in solitude *thinking* about what God wants in your life

I know these goals are very basic. But if we don't keep them, our lives may become a reflex movement, this way and that, in response to an agenda set by others.

[2]Ibid., 71.

Jesus doesn't ask us to seek popularity or to please everyone. *He* certainly didn't. And He doesn't promise that our lives will ever be free of conflicting demands. He faced them constantly, and so will we. But Jesus does call on us to follow Him in learning to make hard choices.

If we follow that path, then at times we will have to say no to others. That's hard. But in freeing ourselves from the treacherous net of other people's demands and expectations, we free ourselves to live for Him in the most effective way possible. Jesus modeled exactly that style of life.

8
What's in It for Me?

In the dark and dreary years of the Great Depression, Kitty McCulloch was known as a generous person. As hunger stalked the land, Kitty and her husband often didn't know for sure about their next week's food, yet a steady stream of hungry men found their back door to ask for a hot meal. And Kitty always gave it to them.

An especially ragged man came near Christmastime one year. Kitty, feeling great pity for him, gave the man one of her husband's few suits. Though she didn't know it for many years, her house had been marked as a message to other needy people that here was a person who cared.

I would define biblical love as a spontaneous desire moving a person to self-giving for the benefit of another. Kitty McCulloch exemplified that kind of love by meeting the needs of others, even when her own resources looked terribly thin.

Jesus Christ modeled such love more than anyone else. He took great personal risks to teach and demonstrate real caring for others. That sets Him in stark contrast to the message our modern world gives to each of us. Culturally we are trained to ask ourselves, "What's in it for *me?*" Jesus faced the very same attitude when He encountered the religious leaders of Israel. On one particular occasion, He confronted them with the ugly truth about their way of living.

CARING ABOUT OTHERS

> One Sabbath, when Jesus went to eat in the house of a promi-
> nent Pharisee, he was being carefully watched. There in front of
> him was a man suffering from dropsy. Jesus asked the Pharisees
> and experts in the law, "Is it lawful to heal on the Sabbath or not?"
> But they remained silent. So taking hold of the man, he healed
> him and sent him away.
> Then he asked them, "If one of you has a son or an ox that falls
> into a well on the Sabbath day, will you immediately pull him
> out?" And they had nothing to say. (Luke 14:1-6)

As Jesus traveled south through Perea on His way to Jerusalem, He was invited to dine with a leading Pharisee, probably a
member of the Sanhedrin. This banquet took place on the Sabbath, the pickiest day of the week. If God made the Sabbath
holy, the Pharisees in their turn made it onerous with the dense
web of legislation they had created to control Sabbath behavior.

Pharisaic theology called upon people to care for others, but
their contemporaries considered them uncaring to a fault. They
generally turned a blind eye toward the poor, the maimed, and
the needy among their people. One story from rabbinic literature should illustrate that quite well. Once a Pharisee encountered a woman drowning in a pond. She died as he looked on,
without making any effort to help. He feared that if he touched
her, he might become ceremonially unclean. You never can tell
about a drowning woman. She might be having her monthly
menstrual discharge, rendering anyone who touched her ceremonially unclean. That might affect the Pharisee's income for a
few days while he remedied his defilement. So, to avoid such
terrible inconvenience, he simply let her drown. Such cases
were not as unusual as one might think.

We know that Jesus had a hostile audience because of the
language used by Luke. He says that Jesus was being "carefully
watched," and this translates a verb that means to lie in wait to
ambush someone. Beneath the external hospitality of this one
man lay the treacherous hook of a trap. The Pharisees earnestly
hoped that Jesus would make a big enough mistake so that He
could be eliminated once and for all.

The Pharisees and scribes had the callousness to use a human
being for bait. How else can we account for the fact that a man
with a debilitating disease would show up for Sabbath lunch
with a member of the Sanhedrin? He was planted there. The

scribes and Pharisees were counting on Jesus' feeling compassion toward this man, in spite of the dangerous context.

The law of Moses permitted miracles to be worked on the Sabbath. However, the super-religious crowd felt that such miracles smacked of working on the Sabbath day, which they abhorred (unless it served their own interests!). These men had no concern for this sick individual; he was simply there as a tool to finesse a miracle out of Jesus. Sitting among the guests were scribes who knew every nook and cranny of the law of Moses as well as the man-made rules that had been added.

Before working the expected miracle, Jesus asked the assembled theologians for a theological opinion about helping others: "Is it lawful to heal on the Sabbath or not?" Perhaps fearing the Lord's well-known abilities, these leaders kept silent. Jesus then healed the sick man in spite of the grave personal risk He was taking in doing so. He knew they would slander Him as someone who had profaned the Sabbath. But such considerations never stopped Jesus. He cared for people even when there was a cost involved.

After sending the healed man away, Jesus confronted the religious leaders with the inconsistency between their own behavior and their super-strict Sabbath rules. Those men could not deny His charge that any one of them would do whatever work was necessary to save his son or his ox on the Sabbath day. The Pharisees would gladly do the very thing they were condemning Jesus for, if their own interests would be served by it. And a Pharisee would not necessarily even save his own son out of love. Their culture had no such thing as Social Security, and a man's sons could be depended upon to support him in his latter years.

I think a better translation of verse 6 would be, "they could make no reply to this." Jesus had them, and they knew it. The hunted had unexpectedly become the hunter.

THE BASIS FOR CARING

When he noticed how the guests picked the places of honor at the table, he told them this parable: "When someone invites you to a wedding feast, do not take the place of honor, for a person more distinguished than you may have been invited. If so, the host who invited both of you will come and say to you, 'Give this man your seat.' Then, humiliated, you will have to take the least important

place. But when you are invited, take the lowest place, so that
when your host comes, he will say to you, 'Friend, move up to a
better place.' Then you will be honored in the presence of all your
fellow guests. For everyone who exalts himself will be humbled,
and he who humbles himself will be exalted." (Luke 14:7-11)

To understand this parable, notice first that the moral is expressed in verse 11. The whole parable drives toward this truth.
Second, observe that the word "but" at the beginning of verse
10 divides the parable into two contrasting halves. Jesus rejected self-exalting behavior in the first half, while He affirmed
humility in the second.

Jesus based the parable on His own observations of guests
taking their places at the table. The Jewish culture used a very
strict pecking order to determine seating assignments at such
banquets. Even in the ranks of the Pharisees some had taken
stricter vows than others and so earned the right to a seat of
higher honor. To give a banquet like that, with a large number
of guests arriving at slightly different times, could involve a
tremendous amount of shuffling around.

Jesus poked fun at this self-serving game of musical chairs.
The whole system was driven by a desire to say to others, "See
how important I am!" Jesus pointedly reminded them that such
self-interested behavior could ultimately result in humiliation if
a more important guest arrived. In fact, the important people in
that society usually did come late so that they could be widely
noticed.

In the second half of the parable, Jesus threw social custom
to the wind by urging the guests to take the lowest seat upon
their arrival. In taking the usual approach, the guest assigns
himself the honor, while the method Jesus described would
involve the host giving the guest an honor. With His story Jesus
said that if you deserve exaltation, let it come from others and
not from yourself.

Jesus capped off the parable with the principle, "He who
humbles himself will be exalted." By whom? God. Jesus cus-
tomarily used the passive voice to express God's actions, as that
was considered preferable to the frequent mention of His name.
God is also the one who will humble the person who exalts
himself.

Unfortunately, I don't think I've ever met a Christian who
wanted to be humble. I can understand that when I consider

the kind of picture people get when we use the word "humble." This word conjures up an image of a person who is so self-effacing that he will hardly even look you in the eye. He feels bad about himself and is so shy that he will never talk to anybody. But that picture bears no resemblance at all to the true likeness of humility. Jesus was a humble person, in the biblical sense of the word, yet He never acted in any of those ways. Humility is not denying our own value, but granting value to others.

GIVING TO OTHERS

> Then Jesus said to his host, "When you give a luncheon or dinner, do not invite your friends, your brothers or relatives, or your rich neighbors; if you do, they may invite you back and so you will be repaid. But when you give a banquet, invite the poor, the crippled, the lame, the blind, and you will be blessed. Although they cannot repay you, you will be repaid at the resurrection of the righteous." (Luke 14:12-14)

A high official like the Sanhedrin leader would have held banquets quite regularly. Invariably such a person would have invited members of his own social class. Strong taboos held the social classes apart from one another. In my opinion, Jesus was not telling the Pharisees (and by application, He is not telling us) that they had to invite someone who was poor, crippled, lame, or blind every time they held a dinner. His real point was that they never showed any concern for such people because of their uncaring attitude. Jesus simply used the example of a banquet because He was sitting at one. It served to illustrate the broader problem.

I find it amusing that Jesus mentioned *"rich* neighbors" (v. 12), because that captured the Pharisaic mentality. A Pharisee might well have *both* rich and poor neighbors, but only the rich neighbor was invited to banquets. Only a rich neighbor could pay the Pharisee back by responding in kind. In this subtle way, Jesus pointed out the inability of the Pharisees to give to others of a lower station than themselves. He was asserting that their whole life revolved around what would ultimately flow back to them in the way of honor, repayment, or social status. Like some members of our own society, the Pharisees were constantly wondering, "What's in it for *me?*"

In the place of their intense self-concern, Jesus exhorted the Pharisees and scribes to meet the needs of others, even if they had to wait until the resurrection of the righteous to receive their repayment. To act that way requires a very farsighted view of life. It won't pay off in the short run.

CARING ABOUT OURSELVES

I hope you will not see what has been said in this chapter as meaning that you ought not to care about yourself. That would simply solve one problem by creating another one. Caring about ourselves is fundamental to spiritual, emotional, and physical health. What the Pharisees did not have, and what Jesus was seeking to give them, was a healthy balance of concern for self and concern for others.

Unfortunately, Christians have sometimes overreacted to the presence of indwelling sin. They have seen self-concern as simply another manifestation of their sin nature. I utterly reject that viewpoint, because each of us is made in the image of God and should therefore be valued accordingly. It is not more spiritual to put a low value on what God values highly.

BALANCING BETWEEN SELF AND OTHERS

Use the following applicational ideas to apply the truth that Jesus taught.
1. In our hurried world, the clock seems to work against us as we try to care for others. The urgent can become the enemy of the important. How do you see yourself, in terms of caring for others?
- Hiding from them
- Overcommitted to them
- Involved with them in a balanced way

It's too easy to hide from people's needs by simply avoiding settings in which we know that their needs will be revealed. Such behavior can betray that we would rather not know about the needs of other people. But, on the other hand, if we overcommit to meeting the needs of others, then we may be overlooking other priorities that God has given to each one of us.

For several decades before 1960, the ruling social ethic in America was to meet the needs of other people and to ignore one's own needs. That may have been what led to a great reaction in the other direction, so that in the 1970s the ruling social ethic became serving oneself. Neither of those positions represents what Jesus wants us to do.

2. Jesus made it quite clear that we should have a healthy concern for the value and needs of others. How do you cope with social status and the needs of others in your own life?

- Do you find yourself quite conscious of someone else's social class, income, education, and so on?

A friend of mine told me a sad story about a prestigious, Christian educational institution. After many years of working there, a man was promoted from one level to a higher level. But he still had friends among his former associations after the promotion. He was soon informed that he could not socialize with those (lower) people anymore. They didn't share his status, so they couldn't share his presence, either. Jesus spoke directly against that kind of thinking.

- Do you find it difficult to roll up your sleeves and go to work in some thankless but vital job?

Every church has vital jobs that go begging because Christians aspire to something "higher." Certainly all of us enjoy recognition, but Jesus said we should be willing to forego immediate rewards and recognition and to wait, if necessary, to be rewarded in eternity. After gaining some experience in the ministry, I now look for people who willingly take such thankless jobs simply because they love Christ. Those are the people I consider most carefully for positions of future leadership.

3. One estimate of our concern for others is whether we can give to them (time, money, a listening ear) without any thought of return.

- When was the last time you gave something to someone who could never repay you?
- When was the last time you gave a gift without concern for what had been or would be given to you by the other person?

My wife was raised in a community in which people did business with one another or favors for one another with the unwritten expectation that the other person would someday reciprocate. No one would actually *say* that such was expected, but everyone knew that it was. There's nothing inherently wrong with that, but it doesn't come anywhere close to what Jesus is talking about when He calls on us to show concern for others.

4. Remember that the person who most needs your caring, serving, and giving may live within your own home. Most of us don't have to look very far to find someone that we can serve, care about, and value.

A FINAL WORD

Edith Evans found someone nearby to serve. She was cruising across the Atlantic, bound for New York from Liverpool on one of the most famous ships of history, the *Titanic*.

Before the *Titanic* sailed, one of the stewards had told a passenger that not even God could sink the ship, which most people aboard had believed as well. But an iceberg struck the *Titanic* and ripped away the forward third of the ship's bottom. The ship began to sink quickly by the bow, while the crew attempted to lower the lifeboats. But over sixteen hundred people had no lifeboat, because the ship had set sail without enough.

Edith Evans and Mrs. John M. Brown showed up at the railing just as the last boat was about to be lowered from the sinking ship. Apart from that boat there was no hope; the dark freezing waters below would kill a person in minutes.

Only one seat remained when the two women got to the rail, and the boat was to be lowered as soon as it was filled. Edith turned to Mrs. Brown and said, "You go first. You have children at home." Edith quickly pushed her over the rail and into the boat just as the deck officer shouted, "Lower away!"

Edith Evans gave up what I would call the seat of honor. The last seat. She had put Mrs. Brown's needs ahead of her own.

Jesus was certainly like that. He gave His life for our sins, not because we deserved it or because we could ever repay Him, but because He loved us that much. Those who follow Him will have lives marked by a balanced concern for others.

9
Wise Nonsense

In this chapter I'm going to try to help you to feel *less* spiritually knowledgeable so that you can learn something. In fact, if I can help you feel as spiritually informed as a seven-year-old, then I will have succeeded beyond my wildest imagination. I am sure that sounds like complete nonsense. But I'm convinced that it's wise nonsense.

You see, there's more than one way to teach and to learn. Jesus once told his disciples, "Anyone who will not receive the kingdom of God like a little child will never enter it" (Mark 10:15). Jesus knew that what His disciples considered *completely* settled about God and about themselves was blocking them from further spiritual growth. He challenged them to become more childlike so that they might grow up in the things of God. Like Jesus' first disciples, we too have absorbed certain erroneous ideas and behaviors that we have cast in personal concrete. Such barriers of the mind must be broken to allow our own spiritual progress.

Jesus often used paradoxes to shatter personal complacency. One expert in biblical literature defines a paradox as "an apparent contradiction which, upon reflection, is seen to express a genuine truth."[1] Paradoxes help us to learn, because they sneak

[1]Leland Ryken, *The Literature of the Bible*, 2d ed. (Grand Rapids: Zondervan, 1980), glossary.

up on us from a totally fresh perspective. They force us to stop
and think like few other techniques can. The title of this chapter, "Wise Nonsense," expresses a paradox. It seems contradic-
tory, because wisdom and nonsense describe opposite ideas. On
reflection, we realize that some truths sound like nonsense but
actually express the very wisdom of God.

Jesus expressed such a truth when He said, "Whoever loses
his life for My sake will find it" (Matthew 11:39). Seeming con-
tradictions abound in His teaching. Such paradoxes give us an
opportunity to go back and become a little more childlike so
that we can see God's truth in a fresh way.

THE RICH MAN'S POVERTY

> As Jesus started on his way, a man ran up to him and fell on his
> knees before him. "Good teacher," he asked, "What must I do to
> inherit eternal life?"
>
> "Why do you call me good?" Jesus answered. "No one is
> good—except God alone. You know the commandments: 'Do not
> murder, do not commit adultery, do not steal, do not give false
> testimony, do not defraud, honor your father and mother.' "
>
> "Teacher," he declared, "all these I have kept since I was a boy."
>
> Jesus looked at him and loved him. "One thing you lack," he
> said. "Go, sell everything you have and give to the poor, and you
> will have treasure in heaven. Then come, follow me."
>
> At this the man's face fell. He went away sad, because he had
> great wealth. (Mark 10:17-22)

With his usual love for vivid action, Mark described a young
man dashing up to Jesus, falling on his knees, and repeatedly
asking Him what personal deeds would lead to eternal life. The
young man's question unveiled the very heart and soul of popular ideas about salvation. First-century Judaism advocated salvation through certain merit-producing works. That would be
salvation by the "merit system." This man wanted to add eternal
life to the bulging portfolio of his wealth.

The Jews considered the Mosaic law a way of earning merit
with God. The Pharisees had listed over six hundred commandments from the law and then had elaborated those even further
to provide additional ways of making points. The Jews imagined a steadily accumulating account of merits that God would
weigh in His balances at the end of a person's life. The law-
abiding Jew fully expected the balance to tip in his favor. On the

other hand, they regarded Gentiles as totally without any prospect of salvation because they lacked a knowledge of God's merit system. That whole concept guided the wording of the rich man's question about eternal life.

Jesus responded to the question in a manner that goes against all we've been told about personal evangelism. But in criticizing the man's question, Jesus began to cut away at the foundational ideas that undergirded it. The man had called Him "Good teacher." Jesus threw the whole idea of human merit into the trash by saying, "No one is good—except God alone."

As long as men think they can attain goodness through human works, they are not ready to attain the only goodness that will ever bring eternal life. Only by renouncing one's own goodness can a person obtain the gift of Christ's goodness through faith. Jesus bluntly shot the man's question out of the sky, because it was hindering his approach to God. In effect, Jesus expressed a paradox: only by denying any merit do we gain merit.

Jesus next focused the man's attention on the commandments of the law. Here the man revealed the depth of his blindness, claiming that he had kept all of the law since he was a boy. He had missed the whole point of the law. A pious Israelite who tried to keep the law would soon realize that he could not possibly do it. His failure would lead him to throw himself upon the mercy of God. But the insidiousness of Pharisaism lay in the fact that it had diluted God's law and made it humanly attainable. Such a heinous deception had captured this man's mind.

In trying to reach this man, Jesus moved him from something hard to something even harder for him. After challenging him with the law, Jesus then confronted him with the need to give away his wealth. Paradoxically, Jesus told the man that he had to give up all of his treasure if he wished to have treasure. That too struck at the foundations of Jewish piety, which taught that charitable gifts, fasting, and prayer were the three best ways of pleasing God. The rich were thought to have heaven "in the bag" because they could dole out little token gifts from their great wealth throughout a lifetime. In fact, the Pharisees specifically forbade anyone from giving away all of his wealth at one time. By asking the man to give away his wealth, Jesus was taking away the best hope for salvation that the man had, according to the thinking of his day. In essence, Jesus told the man that the only way he could get to heaven was to give away the exact thing that he thought would get him there. What wise nonsense! Give away all to gain all.

I think many commentators have misunderstood verse 21, which says, "Jesus looked at him and loved him." It is often said that Jesus felt some special regard for this man. I don't think that's the case at all. Mark was simply telling us that Jesus looked at the man and then loved him in the full biblical sense of the word. Biblical love does not consist of some warm and fuzzy feeling toward someone else, but rather of an act of self-giving for the benefit of another person. Jesus loved this man by revealing to him what was blocking his way to heaven. That is, Jesus' love consisted of action. Paradoxically, His love brought this man shock and sorrow. In verse 22 we are told that "the man's face fell," which means that he was both shocked and appalled by what Jesus had said.

While Jesus was trying to reach through mental barriers to save this rich man, the disciples were standing beside Him, taking it all in. And their heads were beginning to swim with confusion.

POSSIBLE IMPOSSIBILITIES

> Jesus looked around and said to his disciples, "How hard it is for the rich to enter the kingdom of God!"
>
> The disciples were amazed at his words. But Jesus said again, "Children, how hard it is to enter the kingdom of God! It is easier for a camel to go through the eye of a needle than for a rich man to enter the kingdom of God."
>
> The disciples were even more amazed, and said to each other, "Who then can be saved?"
>
> Jesus looked at them and said, "With man this is impossible, but not with God; all things are possible with God." (Mark 10:23-27)

Jesus' first statement hit the disciples like a ton of bricks: "How hard it is for the rich to enter the kingdom of God!" (v. 23). In telling us that, "the disciples were amazed," Mark used a Greek word that means "to be struck." Further, the verb tense indicates that they didn't get over that condition quickly. The word expresses something shattering that happens right in front of your eyes and yet defies belief. Jesus knew that His own disciples held the same erroneous beliefs about wealth as the rich man did.

Jesus then treated the disciples much as He did the rich man, by moving from something hard for them to accept to something even harder. Jesus had them off balance and then knocked them further off balance so that they might learn. With a piece of exaggerated humor, Jesus took the biggest animal in Israel, the camel, and imagined it passing through the smallest opening, the eye of a needle. By implication, Jesus was saying that it is impossible for someone who trusts in riches to enter the kingdom of God.

The effect of Christ's words was to bring His disciples to the point of despair. Mark wrote that the disciples were "even more amazed"; the Greek word means "to be overwhelmed." Jesus had knocked flat all their ideas about wealth. In despair they turned to one another and wondered how anyone could possibly be saved. That idea led to two more paradoxes. The first is that men must reach despair in order to get hope. The disciples had to abandon all hope in the methods of this world so that they might gain the only true hope. Jesus extended that hope to them with another paradox: with God the impossible becomes possible. Their hope did not lie in themselves but in Him.

The entire sequence, including both the rich man and the disciples, expresses a profound paradox about wealth. Wealth seems to men of all ages to bring the greatest security, but that security is deceptive. By relying on wealth, they fail to seek the only security that really does exist, security in God. So, paradoxically, the greatest security brings the greatest peril. Those who have everything stand in the greatest danger of ending life with nothing. Being overwhelmed by Christ's words, the disciples reacted like the rich man. Yet, unlike him, they did not leave Jesus. That illustrates the vast gulf that lay between those who responded to Jesus and those who walked away from Him.

After wiping away the thoughts that His disciples cherished so deeply, Jesus then began to build new ways of thinking. They must leave behind man's patterns and ways of thought, which lead to dead ends of impossibility. They must instead trust in the Lord, with whom all things become possible (see also Matthew 19:26; Luke 18:27).

THE LAST FIRST

> Peter said to him, "We have left everything to follow you!"
> "I tell you the truth," Jesus replied, "no one who has left home or brothers or sisters or mother or father or children or fields for

> me and the gospel will fail to receive a hundred times as much in
> this present age (homes, brothers, sisters, mothers, children and
> fields—and with them, persecutions) and in the age to come,
> eternal life. But many who are first will be last, and the last first."
> (Mark 10:28-31)

Quite understandably, Peter sought reassurance from Jesus.
In reply, Jesus acknowledged that His disciples had given up
both families and inheritances for His sake. As a result, they
would win the grand prize. Paradoxically, they forsook all to
receive even more in its place. Those who seem according to
the standards of the world to have it made, those using the
world's patterns, will in fact be last in the age to come. By
contrast, the disciples of Jesus, whom the religious establish-
ment considered to be the last, will prove in the age to come to
be the children of the Father, and therefore the first of all.

Paul puts it in another way in 1 Corinthians 1. The world
considers the cross foolishness, but the foolishness of God is
wiser than man's wisdom. The very thing the world considers
laughable is the thing that God will use to save those who will
put their faith in His Son. Paradoxically, through death (at the
cross) comes life (for all who believe).

I hope that you can see how Jesus used paradoxes to get His
disciples to think new thoughts about God. He knocked them
off balance and brought them to the point of despair so that they
might find the only true hope.

BECOMING CHILDISH ADULTS IN CHRIST

I want to apply this passage by asking you to rethink some
things in a manner similar to the way Jesus asked His own
disciples to rethink. In setting aside long-established ideas, we
can become more like children for a little while, and more
pliable in Christ's hands. Use the following ideas to guide you:
1. One of our greatest needs is to develop Christ's viewpoint on
life's complex issues. As you study the Scriptures, here are two
suggestions:

- Meditate the most on the verses you like the least. Doesn't
  that sound like fun? Such behavior would be paradoxical,
  and it would have a significant purpose. What God says
  that you find the most uncomfortable of all is probably the
  very point at which the theological system in your head
  needs to be changed.

- Look for situations in which Jesus behaves in a way that would feel embarrassing or very unnatural for you.

Remember how Jesus treated the unsaved young man. He didn't "evangelize" him the way any contemporary believer would. What can we learn from that? In teaching His disciples, Jesus first knocked them off balance and then knocked them totally down! What can we learn from that, in terms of teaching and learning in our own lives? By carefully evaluating such unusual approaches, we can pick up profound insights about our own ways of doing things. Such situations certainly should lead us to wonder whether we derive our own patterns of behavior from our surrounding culture or from Jesus Himself.

2. Things are not always what they seem to be. Wealth and accomplishment can deceive us by promising something they cannot deliver. Wealth promises security, but there is no lasting security except in the Lord.

Great or numerous accomplishments can deceive us into thinking that we are doing something of lasting value. But only those actions that serve Christ, His people, and His kingdom will truly endure and be rewarded.

Thousands of years ago, three pharaohs each erected a great pyramid outside of Cairo. These tremendous monuments of achievement took over twenty years to build. Can you personally name a single one of these men? Can you imagine putting forth such tremendous effort without any eternal value whatsoever?

- Where is your security based? Is it based in your bank account?
- Will your busy actions stand the test of time?

I'm certainly not striking against work or saying that the only way to please God is to be involved in some *church* activity. Whatever work we do, we will be eternally rewarded when we do that work as unto the Lord (see Colossians 3:23). So I am not saying that our work is wrong or unimportant. But I am saying that we need to relate our work and the energy of our lives to serving the kingdom of God. Only that focus will prove of maximum value in the age to come.

3. Some of the things that the Lord calls on us to do bring us struggle, because our life experiences cry out, "that won't work!" But the very essence of living by faith is doing things His way even when we cannot see what the consequences will be. The rich man considered Christ's ideas nonsense. By contrast,

the disciples were willing to follow Him even when they couldn't see where the road might lead.

4. What are your two greatest strengths, personally or spiritually? I want you to think of something concrete about yourself and even to write it down. Are you reliable, loving, or intelligent? What do people value about you? Are you giving, articulate, or kind?

When I filled in those blanks, I put down knowledge first. A great deal of my life has focused on accumulating and teaching knowledge. But, you know, there is something paradoxical about knowledge, because Jesus couldn't teach the scribes anything. They already considered themselves so smart that they didn't think there was anything that an untutored teacher from Galilee could tell them.

In the second blank I wrote another strong point of mine— the fact that I work very hard. I generally do what has to be done and get the job done. Even so, a friend of mine pointed out the other day that work is about the *only* thing I do. He stumped me when he said, "What do you do to play?" I'm seldom at a loss for words, but I really stumbled around with that one. I couldn't come up with much except for things that I do once a year on vacation. He pointed out that because I do not have a proper balance of work and play in my own life, I'm not in a position to teach either my children or the people in my church a healthy style of living. I felt like I had just been had!

Here's the point: Have you considered the seemingly absurd possibility that your greatest strengths may be your areas of greatest weakness in your walk with Christ? What you do best may need some rethinking and readjustment. The purpose of that is not to do away with your strengths, but to keep them from becoming your greatest weaknesses.

As believers we need to be willing to open every door of our lives, including those areas that we consider totally settled. We need to reevaluate even our greatest strengths so that Jesus can make us ever more effective for Him.

A FINAL WORD

As strange as it may sound, I hope I have helped you feel less certain about the Lord, about yourself, and about how to live for Christ. If you feel a little more like a child, a little off balance, I think that's good.

I enjoy downhill skiing. I find it exhilarating to ski up to a steep place and look down. The thing that's tough about it is that the way to ski a steep run is to lean downhill and begin to pick up speed. That doesn't sound right, does it! To go that fast is scary and seems like the last thing you would want to do. But paradoxically, up to a certain point, the faster your skis go, the more control they can give you. And so, what feels like the worst thing you can do is actually the thing that can bring you the most stability and control.

So if you feel a little off balance by what has been said, don't fight it. Take your uncertainty and your new concerns right where a child should go—to the Father. Study His Word. Pray for renewed wisdom. What you will find is that Jesus will take your weakened convictions and rebuild them, just as He did for His disciples.

10

A Big Difference

Years ago I made a large astronomical telescope, which has provided me with hours of fun. Whenever I set up my telescope in the front yard, it takes about fifteen minutes to draw a crowd. As people walk up, they see a large cylinder pointed up toward the sky. Invariably, someone will go around behind the telescope, crouch down, and look up through the bottom, expecting to catch a glimpse of the heavens. It shocks them to realize that they can't see a thing!

You see, anyone who grows up in America develops a general concept of how telescopes work. Through limited experience they develop the idea that you use every telescope by looking in one straight line through the optics to the target. That holds true for *most* telescopes, but not for mine. The eyepiece on my telescope is on the side, near the front. To observe with me, people have to give up their time-honored ideas about how telescopes work. They must use my telescope according to its unique (Newtonian) design.

Sometimes the way we look at things makes a big difference indeed. I'm personally convinced that our principle of looking at things in culturally conditioned ways applies to the way we see the church and its leaders. Having grown up in America, the great majority of us have become accustomed to thinking of the church as working in a totally different way from the way

Jesus Christ designed it. So the church often doesn't function as
it should. Even its leaders don't follow the role that Christ intended; they too are caught up in the cultural pattern. That
makes a big difference.

The most critical gospel passage on church leadership comes
from Mark 10. This passage also illustrates why the authors of
the gospels sometimes put stories side by side. At first glance,
many of these stories may seem unrelated, but further study
will reveal a strong connection. Such is the case in Mark 10.

Mark's account flows through three stages of thought. In the
first the focus is on serving self, strictly catering to one's pleasures. The second part stresses serving other people, by placing
other people's interests ahead of one's own. The final stage
involves serving God, putting His will above and before all else.

A FAULTY DESIGN

> Then James and John, the sons of Zebedee, came to him.
> "Teacher," they said, "we want you to do for us whatever we ask."
> "What do you want me to do for you?" he asked.
> They replied, "Let one of us sit at your right and the other at
> your left in your glory."
> "You don't know what you are asking," Jesus said. "Can you
> drink the cup I drink or be baptized with the baptism I am bap-
> tized with?"
> "We can," they answered.
> Jesus said to them, "You will drink the cup I drink and be
> baptized with the baptism I am baptized with, but to sit at my
> right or left is not for me to grant. These places belong to those for
> whom they have been prepared." (Mark 10:35-40)

Those events probably took place on the east side of the
Jordan River as Jesus and His disciples journeyed south toward
Jerusalem. It may have been during a brief rest stop that James
and John made their play for power. They began with one of the
most open-ended requests in the history of the world: "We want
you to do for us *whatever we ask*" (v. 35, italics added). When
they got down to specifics, they were asking for the number two
and number three positions in the kingdom of God. They wanted to be the second and third most powerful people in all
eternity.

The other gospels inform us that, at that point, James and
John still thought Jesus would set up the millennial kingdom

very soon. They believed that the trip to Jerusalem would conclude with His glorious reign. I don't really know why they
expected that, because Jesus told them repeatedly what would
actually happen. He was going to Jerusalem to die. From their
request, we can plainly see that His plans did not fit into theirs.

Some days before the approach by James and John, the disciples had argued vehemently among themselves (Mark 9:33-34).
Jesus later asked them what they had argued about, but none of
them wanted to tell Him. They were ashamed to admit that they
had fought over who was the greatest among them.

Their self-interest had not gone away. That's why James and
John reasserted their claims. They were trying to sneak in front
of the other ten by asking Jesus for those privileges first. Such
tactics would have been logical, had they been serving in the
court of King Herod, that master of political intrigue. That's the
way the game is played in this world's councils of power. But
James and John had totally misunderstood the design of
Christ's ministry.

In responding to James and John, Jesus tried in several ways
to point them in the opposite direction (v. 38). He even asked
them a question that had a built-in answer! The Greek language
has a technique for telling the listener what answer is expected.
And so, Christ's question means, "You can't drink the cup I
drink or be baptized with the baptism that I am baptized with,
can you?" To drink someone's cup means to share his fate, in
this case, death on a Roman cross. To be baptized means to be
overwhelmed or engulfed, in this case by God's wrath against
sin that would engulf the Son of God. But James and John
demonstrated their lack of spiritual insight and the keenness of
their self-interest by ignoring the prompted answer Jesus had
given them. They said, "We can." They were willing to do whatever was necessary to gain power.

Jesus then predicted that they *would* experience part of His
suffering. (In A.D. 44, James was martyred by Herod Agrippa.
John was ultimately banished to the island of Patmos in the
Mediterranean, from which he wrote Revelation.) Next, Jesus
flatly denied the two brothers' request by saying that those
places of honor "belong to those for whom they have been
prepared." In my view, Jesus didn't have anyone specific in
mind; He was speaking of a certain *kind* of person. A little later
He described the kind of person that would receive that coveted
honor.

> When the ten heard about this, they became indignant with James and John. Jesus called them together and said, "You know that those who are regarded as rulers of the Gentiles lord it over them, and their high officials exercise authority over them. Not so with you. Instead, whoever wants to become great among you must be your servant, and whoever wants to be first must be slave of all. For even the Son of Man did not come to be served, but to serve, and to give His life as a ransom for many." (Mark 10:41-45)

The two brothers' power politics soon blew up in their faces. The other seekers-after-status learned what had happened and became "indignant" with the two. This word means to be angry at some impropriety. In trying to sneak in ahead of all the others, James and John hadn't played by the rules. The other ten apostles actually wanted the same thing James and John did, but they didn't get off of the starting blocks quite as quickly. So in the midst of His solemn journey to Jerusalem, where He was to suffer so terribly, Christ had to straighten out the twelve men in whom He had invested the most.

Jesus cut straight to the heart of their problem. They had totally misunderstood His design for the relationships among his followers. They had drawn their model for behavior from the surrounding pagan world. The rulers of the Gentiles "lord it over them"; the Greek verb has the clear nuance of self-interest. The Herods and Caesars did not rule in the interest of those being governed, but solely for their own purposes. Their kingdoms functioned for maximum personal benefit. In the Roman world, the high officials "exercised authority" over others, again with the implication of self-interest and exploitation. The whole power structure of the Gentile world served the interests of the people at the top, at the expense of the people on the bottom.

We should understand that, because we live in a world just like that. Like James and John, we have all grown accustomed to it and think that such power structures are normal. Within their cultural context, the request of James and John made complete sense, but they had drawn their model for the body of Christ from culture.

In response to that viewpoint, Jesus uttered four of the most important words in the New Testament: "Not so with you" (Mark 10:43). With this firm and simple statement, Jesus wiped the top-down model of power right off the blackboard. Those who follow Jesus must adopt a totally different design. Jesus then described what it takes to be great in the body of Christ (vv. 43-44). To be *great* involves voluntary service on behalf of others, which is the underlying meaning of the Greek noun translated "servant." To be *first* in the body of Christ, as James and John wanted to be, requires even more. Such a person must be the "slave" of all. The Greek word refers to a person who has completely subjected his own interests to the interests of another.

Instead of drawing their model from the world, the disciples should have watched Jesus, who put His own interests aside. Christ voluntarily set aside the privileges of heaven to come to our world and share our struggle. Paul tells us that Jesus condescended to come in the very form of a slave (Philippians 2:7). God was trying to teach us something by the way that His Son came into the world. His message to us was totally countercultural and goes against the designs that we've all grown so accustomed to. But *among us* Jesus wants a different design, and leaders are to function there in a completely different way.

A MISSED OPPORTUNITY

Now I want to give you a brief exposition of what is *not* written in the biblical text at this point. Mark should happily have said that James and John repented of their extreme self-interest and bad attitude. But we don't read that, do we? They seemed unaffected by what Jesus had said.

And what would you expect Jesus to have done, in light of their lack of response? We might guess that Jesus would rebuke them and tell them that He was going to *make* them act like servants. He had the power to make them act any way He wanted. Jesus had both the power and the right to do that, but He knew that would be a violation of the very principles He was trying to teach them. It would have violated His design for the body of Christ, the church.

The church does not function by its leaders' forcing others to do what they are supposed to do. Jesus didn't work that way, either. He did exactly what He wanted later Christian leaders to do: after teaching others by word, He taught them by personal example.

> Then they came to Jericho. As Jesus and his disciples, together with a large crowd, were leaving the city, a blind man, Bartimaeus (that is, the Son of Timaeus), was sitting by the roadside begging. When he heard that it was Jesus of Nazareth, he began to shout, "Jesus, Son of David, have mercy on me!"
>
> Many rebuked him and told him to be quiet, but he shouted all the more, "Son of David, have mercy on me!"
>
> Jesus stopped and said, "Call him."
>
> So they called to the blind man, "Cheer up! On your feet! He's calling you." Throwing his cloak aside, he jumped to his feet and came to Jesus.
>
> "What do you want me to do for you?" Jesus asked him.
>
> The blind man said, "Rabbi, I want to see."
>
> "Go," said Jesus, "your faith has healed you." Immediately he received his sight and followed Jesus along the road. (Mark 10:46-52)

After teaching His disciples in a private setting, Jesus modeled for them in a public setting. Because Jesus was near Jericho, a large crowd had gathered around Him. As the crowd walked along the road with Christ, suddenly one of Israel's many blind men cried out. Most blind men probably would have welcomed a crowd as an opportunity to receive alms, but Bartimaeus was not like others. He had heard that Jesus of Nazareth was coming.

Bartimaeus began to shout, "Jesus, *Son of David*, have mercy on me!" Think carefully; Nazareth is not the city of David. So Bartimaeus must have known more about Jesus than the average blind man did. He apparently understood who Jesus was and what He had come to do ("have mercy"). He didn't ask Him for position or power, but for something in keeping with the design and purpose of Christ's mission. James and John had requested something at cross purposes to Christ's mission, and they had been denied it. Jesus didn't come to hand out seats of power, but to show the mercy of God.

For his trouble, Bartimaeus received nothing but flak. The crowd, the disciples, and (I would be willing to guarantee you) the Twelve joined together to rebuke the man. In effect, they said, "Shut up! Keep quiet. The Great Man doesn't have time to fool around with the likes of you. Don't you know He's going to Jerusalem to do something important?" They considered it improper for a blind man to halt Jesus on His holy mission. But

Bartimaeus understood the design of Christ's life far better than the multitude or the disciples did. He simply cried out all the more, "Son of David, have mercy on me!"

At this, Jesus stopped dead in His tracks, and the whole multitude must have gradually ground to a halt. The Son of God, on His way to atone for the sins of the world, paused to meet the needs of one blind beggar. By His example, Jesus showed that He came to serve and not to be served.

Christ instructed those around Him to call the blind man. Then the mood of the entire group changed, and the people began to encourage the blind man. When Jesus called him, Bartimaeus demonstrated all of the spiritual insight and faith that James and John had previously lacked. He threw his cloak aside and quickly approached Christ to make his request. In a matter of seconds, his eyesight was restored.

Consider what this man had done even before he approached Jesus. He had *thrown his cloak aside!* It gets cold in the Jericho valley at night, and he undoubtedly would have needed that cloak to survive. The poor often had to depend on such garments for shelter, because they couldn't afford a house. I can't prove it, but I suggest that Bartimaeus threw his cloak aside because he knew that in a few moments he would be able to find it with no trouble. He believed that Jesus would grant his request.

Consider too why Bartimaeus wanted to see. He didn't use the gift for his own interests. He immediately began to follow Jesus with his newfound eyesight. He wanted to use it to serve God and not just himself. The other gospels tell us that he gave praise to God along the way.

A BACKWARD GLANCE

By placing these two incidents side-by-side, Mark made his point powerfully. The section begins with two men who were serving themselves. Jesus rebuked them and taught that anyone who wants to become great among His followers must put the interests of others ahead of his own. Jesus then modeled this principle, with the result that men praised God. Selfish interest leads to quarreling and bickering, but serving others in a balanced way leads to the glory of God.

James and John failed to understand the design of relationships among the followers of Jesus Christ. They lacked spiritual insight and drew their model from the world. By contrast, Bartimaeus understood what Jesus had come to do and tailored his request to fit that. As a result, Bartimaeus came away a big winner. It makes a big difference to follow the design that Jesus has given.

Finally, I think these incidents amply demonstrate how leaders ought to function within the body of Christ. Not only should they set aside any interest in power and status, but they should also realize that they will not accomplish Christ's goals by commanding and controlling others. Jesus taught first by word and then by the model of His own life. He expects leaders in the body of Christ to follow the same pattern.

A BIG DIFFERENCE IN THE CHURCH

The main arena for applying the truth of this passage is the local church. Many Christians think the church and its leaders should function just like American corporations, because that's the cultural pattern they have seen. On top is the pastor, with the highest authority; on the next layer down is the church board; and underneath that lies the individual member. We can diagram such a church in the following way:

Chart 6

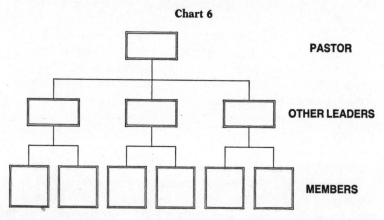

This arrangement is not evil. It's not wrong for businesses and organizations to structure themselves this way. But Jesus said that it is "not to be so with you." Jesus rejected this power-structure model, which is so prevalent in the world, and said that it has no place among His followers. The body of Christ, the church, should be organized very differently from any other type of group. And that is very hard to get used to. It violates our culture as greatly as it did the culture of James and John.

The spiritual leader, as described in the New Testament, has a totally different kind of authority, which he exercises by *teaching* and *example*. Peter said, "To the elders among you, I appeal as a fellow elder . . . be shepherds of God's flock . . . not lording it over those entrusted to you, but being *examples* to the flock" (1 Peter 5:1-3, italics added). Peter did not throw his apostolic authority around, as he could have; instead, he appealed to his fellow elders. That style of leadership leaves each individual believer with a high degree of freedom in, and responsibility to, the Lord. (The interested reader should also study the more technical appendix to this chapter, in which I discuss 1 Timothy 3:4-5.)

In presenting the following chart, I want to acknowledge my indebtedness to Dr. Larry Richards, who first introduced me to these ideas.

Chart 7			
TYPE OF AUTHORITY	**EXAMPLES**	**FREEDOM**	**RESULT**
Position (right to *direct*)	Employer to worker Parent to child	Some	External comformity
Servant (right to *influence*)	Elder to church member Adult to adult Professional-client	High	Inner commitment

The *position* type of authority represents what we commonly encounter in our culture. A good illustration of this is the relationship between an employer and his subordinate. Here the worker has some freedom; after all, he can always quit. But usually that's too high a price to pay. Normally the worker simply follows the direction that is given him. In other words, he externally conforms to what he's told to do. This is a *control style of leadership*.

But the control style has no place in the church. In the body of Christ, the *servant* type of authority should be used, as described in the second line. By analogy, Jesus taught that spiritual leaders should relate to others in a manner culturally similar to the way a professional would relate to a client. Or the way a doctor relates to a patient.

Not long ago a very capable doctor told me that I ought to lose weight. He had all the authority of medical research and good sense behind him, but he couldn't *make* me lose that weight. I could have told him to forget it. He has no control over me. But he does have a right to influence my thinking and behavior. A wise response on my part would have been to voluntarily follow his advice, which I did. On my part, the degree of freedom in that relationship was high. I arrived at an inner commitment to the advice my doctor had given me. (And I lost the weight!)

In a similar way, spiritual leaders have the right to influence others in the church by their teaching and example. A wise believer will carefully consider their input. Christians should listen to spiritual leaders, not because those leaders have a right to control behavior, but because God's people should be influenced by those who know His principles and live according to them. It's not a matter of compulsion.

Christ's counter-cultural model of spiritual leadership leads to a situation within the church that could be diagrammed in the following way:

Chart 7a

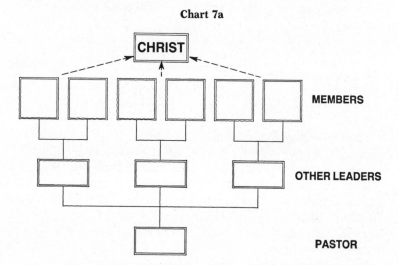

Again, I have borrowed this idea from Dr. Larry Richards. To me it fits exactly what Jesus was teaching His disciples about the way the church should function. The leader should support, nurture, facilitate, and care for the people in such a way that they look to Christ for direction. Human leaders should *not* be the focal point of the local church. That role is reserved for Jesus, the Lord of the church.

"BUT..."

Americans are a wonderfully pragmatic people. A common question that arises at this point is: "Will servant-leadership work?" In my view, that isn't the real issue. The real issue is whether we will individually respond to Christ and His Word, as taught and modeled by our spiritual leaders, or draw our design for the church from the culture around us.

A FINAL WORD

Several years ago, a problem developed deep under Cheyenne Mountain near Colorado Springs. This granite giant houses the North American Air Defense Command and contains huge electronic display screens that signal the onset of any Soviet military threat. One morning, a screen lit up suddenly indicating that two submarine-launched ballistic missiles were headed for the American east coast—Washington, D.C., Philadelphia, or some other major city might only have a few minutes to live. Signals immediately went out to American defense forces all over the world. Our bomber forces launched their armed flights to retaliate. At about that time, the attack signal vanished from the screen. It disappeared as quickly as it had come.

Later, technicians discovered that within the computer a forty-nine-cent part had malfunctioned and reported an attack when in fact there had been none. That tiny part nearly changed world history.

Perhaps what our churches need is a small change that will produce a big difference. What we need, for the church to function as Christ designed it, is a small but crucial change in each of our hearts. I think it boils down to a willingness to do things *His* way, rather than the way *we* think they should be done.

APPENDIX TO CHAPTER 10

Beyond any question, we must consider 1 Timothy 3:4-5 in establishing how leaders should function within the body of

Christ. Here Paul discussed one of the qualifications for elder-
ship. The *New International Version* provides the following
translation of these verses:

> He must *manage*[1] his own family well and see that his children
> obey him with proper respect. (If anyone does not know how to
> *manage*[2] his own family, how can he *take care of*[3] God's church?)

Translators grow up in cultures and sometimes make their
translation choices based upon what they have become accustomed to in those particular cultures. I believe that has happened here in the *New International Version*.

To help you understand the choices the translators have
made, I would like to provide for you the alternate meanings of
the three Greek verbs used in this passage. The verb *prohistemi*
means either (1) "be at the head of, rule, direct, manage," or
(2) "be concerned about, care for." Obviously, the first meaning
has a more authoritarian flavor, while the latter meaning has
more of an emphasis on nurturing and support. The key question is this: which meaning should the translator choose for this
particular context? The *New International Version* translators
have chosen the first meaning, and I think they have done so
based upon their own cultural backgrounds. I prefer the latter
meaning, for reasons that will be given below.

The Greek verb *epimelomai* has only one meaning: "care for,
take care of." The meaning of this verb provides the solution to
the entire translation problem. The logic of verses 4 and 5
demands that all three verbs mean *the same thing*. Therefore,
the verb with the narrowest meaning will control the other two.
Because of those facts, we must use *epimelomai* to give us the
proper meaning of *prohistemi*. In both cases, the proper meaning is "care for, take care of."

These considerations lead to the following translation:

> He must care for his own family well and see that his children
> obey him with proper respect. (If anyone does not know how to
> care for his own family, how can he care for God's church?)

To some readers it may seem that this change in translation is

---

[1]The Greek verb *prohistemi.*
[2]The Greek verb *prohistemi.*
[3]The Greek verb *epimelomai.*

not worth talking about. However, these verses are frequently used to legitimize the use of management practices from American corporations in the local church. Yet that is exactly what Jesus said we must *not* do. If the local church functions as Jesus designed it to function, then leaders will not "manage" the church, but will instead care for it and take care of the people within it. That is the servant-leader model of biblical leadership.

11

Stress Test

Vera Menchik found the whole thing quite amusing. It all started when she became the first woman to play in an international chess tournament. Few chess tournaments either before or since have gathered such an array of stars—all men.

But some of the men didn't think Vera belonged at the tournament. In particular, a master named Albert Becker declared before the tournament that if anyone lost a game to her, they ought to be forced to join the Vera Menchik Fan Club. As it turned out, poor Vera won only one game. She met and defeated Albert Becker. He became the first member of the Vera Menchik Fan Club!

That story both amuses and pleases us because we have a God-given sense of justice. We feel closure when the punishment so beautifully fits the crime.

But things don't always turn out like that. Justice is not always done. I'm sure you've seen at least one grade B western in which the leader of a lynch mob glances with cold rage at an unfortunate prisoner and says, "We're going to give this man a fair trial and then hang him." That almost intuitively raises a note of fear within us, because we realize that justice is being thrown to the winds. Unfortunately, that perverted kind of "justice" prevailed on April 3, A.D. 33 in the trial of Jesus Christ.[1]

---

[1]Harold W. Hoehner, *Chronological Aspects of the Life of Christ* (Grand Rapids: Zondervan, 1976), 114.

KANGAROO COURT

On the previous night, Thursday, Jesus had observed the Pass-over with His disciples, a time we refer to as the Last Supper. Before the celebration had run its course, Judas left the group to consummate his betrayal of Jesus to the Jewish religious leaders. After singing a psalm to conclude the Passover meal, Jesus and the others crossed over into the garden of Gethsema-ne. As He was arrested there, Jesus said to His captors, "This is your hour—when darkness reigns" (Luke 22:53).

Through that long night, Jesus faced the mock justice of a kangaroo court composed of the leaders who had plotted His death and held in the home of Caiaphas the high priest. On the way toward their certain verdict, they broke literally dozens of the Sanhedrin's laws regarding trials. Their own laws accused them of perverting justice, but in Christ's case they went right ahead. When they had reached the appointed verdict, they took Jesus at about dawn to the headquarters of Pontius Pilate, the Roman prefect.

INTO THE PRESSURE COOKER

In the early morning stillness, the Sanhedrin brought Jesus under the foreboding walls of the Antonia Fortress. The fortress covered an area about the size of Yankee Stadium and had walls over seventy-five feet high. In this imposing structure, sur-rounded by his own Roman troops, Pilate stood, ready to meet any disturbance that might arise during the Passover celebra-tion. I find it ironic that, in such a position of power, it was Pilate who would come under enormous pressure and would ultimately crumble.

You see, the Jews had to bring tremendous pressure on Pilate to accomplish their goal of putting Jesus to death. The Romans had wisely kept to themselves the right to execute criminals so that civil leaders couldn't start trouble through rash actions. The Sanhedrin also faced the double difficulty that Jesus had done nothing wrong and that they could not show any breach of Roman law.

Very little survives from Roman times down to our present day, but the rigorous Roman legal system has profoundly influ-enced our own forms of justice. To accomplish their goal, the Sanhedrin knew that they would have to put such enormous pressures on Pilate that he would be forced to violate the legal system he had sworn to uphold.

The Jews accused Jesus of three things before Pilate (see Luke 23:2-5): (1) opposing payment of taxes to Caesar, (2) stirring up the people by His teaching, and (3) claiming to be Messiah, a king. Pilate totally ignored the first two charges. He knew that Christ's teaching had not led to any insurrection. Knowing the Roman sensitivity to possible trouble, we can surmise that Pilate's agents had heard what Jesus said about rendering to Caesar that which was Caesar's (see Matthew 22:21). Accordingly, Pilate knew that Jesus had not made any attempt to subvert the taxation system. Only the charge about kingship gave Pilate any concern at all. As Caesar's agent, Pilate had to ensure that no person set up his own authority in opposition to Roman authority. For anyone to do that would constitute high treason, punishable by the death penalty.

AN OPEN AND SHUT CASE

> Pilate then went back inside the palace, summoned Jesus and asked him, "Are you the king of the Jews?"
>
> "Is that your own idea," Jesus asked, "or did others talk to you about me?"
>
> "Do you think I am a Jew?" Pilate replied. "It was your people and your chief priests who handed you over to me. What is it you have done?"
>
> Jesus said, "My kingdom is not of this world. If it were, my servants would fight to prevent my arrest by the Jews. But now my kingdom is from another place."
>
> "You are a king, then!" said Pilate.
>
> Jesus answered, "You are right in saying I am a king. In fact, for this reason I was born, and for this I came into the world, to testify to the truth. Everyone on the side of truth listens to me."
>
> "What is truth?" Pilate asked. With this he went out again to the Jews and said, "I find no basis for a charge against him." (John 18:33-38)

Christ's Roman trial began quietly enough. Pilate seemed unruffled and in complete command of the situation. Jesus, in spite of the fact that His life was at stake, betrayed no hint of fear or concern about the outcome. He cogently observed that if He were the kind of king that Pilate was concerned about, then His followers would be fighting for Him at that moment.

Pilate hardly needed to concern himself with a kingdom that was "not of this world."

Pilate continued to press Jesus on the central issue of His kingship. By admitting He was a king only under direct question from Pilate, Jesus demonstrated that He was not flaunting His right to rule in opposition to Rome. All of the initiative on that subject had originated with Pilate. At the end of His remarks, Jesus beautifully took the offense by saying, "Everyone on the side of truth listens to me." Implicitly He was asking whether Pilate was on the side of truth. But the mighty prefect had come to ask questions, not to answer them, so he contemptuously swept the matter aside. The quiet phase of Christ's Roman trial ended with Pilate's declaring Jesus innocent of all charges. Before the whole matter ended, Pilate would pronounce Jesus innocent three different times, but He was still executed.

Because Jesus was innocent, we ought to be told that He was set free. But the fact that Pilate, who held supreme power in Palestine, did not release Christ has caused controversy for many years. Recent research into this period of history has provided a satisfying explanation.[2]

In his early years as prefect, Pilate had treated the Jews quite brutally and had done whatever he pleased. How then could he appear as such a weak and vacillating figure, allowing an innocent man to be crucified? The answer lies in Pilate's relationship to Roman central authority. During all of the years of Pilate's role as prefect, Tiberius ruled as Roman emperor. However, Tiberius bordered on insanity and isolated himself on the island of Capri. He ruled through deputies and seldom took a direct part in the everyday affairs of the Empire. The real power behind the throne during those years was a man named Lucius Sejanus, the head of the Imperial Guards. It was he who appointed Pilate as prefect in A.D. 26. Sejanus hated the Jews and undoubtedly backed Pilate's harsh measures against them.

But in A.D. 31, Tiberius had Sejanus executed and began to take a stronger role in the affairs of the Empire. Late in that year he issued orders that the Jews should not be mistreated. And in A.D. 32 Tiberius reversed certain actions that Pilate had taken toward the Jews.

So by the time Jesus came to trial before Pilate, the prefect was skating on very thin ice with Tiberius. Any trouble with the

[2]Ibid., 111-12.

Jews could result in his immediate dismissal, as it would seem he was violating Tiberius's command not to mistreat the Jews. Because of Pilate's tenuous political situation, the Jewish leaders knew exactly where to apply pressure on him. The following chart summarizes the historical background of the trial.

		Chart 8	
		Roman History and the Trial	
	A.D. 26	Pilate appointed prefect by Sejanus	
October	A.D. 31	Sejanus executed	
Late	A.D. 31	Tiberius's order not to mistreat Jews	
	A.D. 32	Pilate reversed by Tiberius	
April	A.D. 33	Jesus tried before Pilate	

AN ATTEMPT TO WIGGLE OUT

"But it is your custom for me to release to you one prisoner at the time of the Passover. Do you want me to release 'the king of the Jews?' "

They shouted back, "No, not him! Give us Barabbas!" Now Barabbas had taken part in a rebellion.

Then Pilate took Jesus and had him flogged. The soldiers twisted together a crown of thorns and put it on his head. They clothed him in a purple robe and went up to him again and again, saying, "Hail, O king of the Jews!" And they struck him in the face.

Once more Pilate came out and said to the Jews, "Look, I am bringing him out to you to let you know that I find no basis for a charge against him." When Jesus came out wearing the crown of thorns and the purple robe, Pilate said to them, "Here is the man!"

As soon as the chief priests and their officials saw him, they shouted, "Crucify! Crucify!"

But Pilate answered, "You take him and crucify him. As for me, I find no basis for a charge against him." (John 18:39—19:6)

Knowing that the Sanhedrin wanted Jesus to die, Pilate tried to maneuver around them by appealing to the Passover crowds. He first attempted to release the popular teacher, in accordance with a custom that had long been followed at Passover. But by working hard among the crowd, the leaders thwarted this attempt and prompted the crowd to call for the release of Barabbas, a common thief.

The Aramaic name *Barabbas* means "son of the father." The guilty son of a human father was released, while the innocent Son of the divine Father was condemned to death. That irony highlights the miscarriage of justice that occurred.

Frustrated in his first attempt to free Jesus, Pilate then tried a second stratagem. He would have Jesus reduced to a bleeding, savagely beaten state and bring him back before the crowd in hopes they would feel pity for their fellow countryman. To carry out this plan he had Jesus flogged with a Roman whip. How understated the gospel account is! A Roman whip normally had pieces of glass, bone, and metal tied in the strips of leather so that every blow would tear the victim's skin open.

In mockery of His claims to be a king, the soldiers gave Jesus a crown of thorns and then greeted Him in a way similar to the way a person would greet Caesar. Matthew and Luke tell us that after issuing these greetings, they beat Christ across the head with rods. What a sight Jesus must have been when Pilate declared Him innocent the second time and then had Him hauled out before the multitude. But the moment Jesus came into sight, the leaders again incited a shout that Jesus should be crucified. Pilate was becoming more desperate by the moment.

THE FINAL CRUNCH

> The Jews insisted, "We have a law, and according to that law he must die, because he claimed to be the Son of God."
>
> When Pilate heard this, he was even more afraid, and he went back inside the palace. "Where do you come from?" he asked Jesus, but Jesus gave him no answer. "Do you refuse to speak to me?" Pilate said. "Don't you realize I have power either to free you or to crucify you?"
>
> Jesus answered, "You would have no power over me if it were not given to you from above. Therefore the one who handed me over to you is guilty of a greater sin."
>
> From then on, Pilate tried to set Jesus free, but the Jews kept shouting, "If you let this man go, you are no friend of Caesar. Anyone who claims to be a king opposes Caesar."
>
> When Pilate heard this, he brought Jesus out and sat down on the judge's seat at a place known as The Stone Pavement (which in Aramaic is Gabbatha). (John 19:7-13)

In the grip of a moment of emotion, the Jews finally unveiled before Pilate their *real* reason for wanting Christ's death: He had claimed to be the Son of God. If Pilate had had any remaining doubt about Christ's innocence, that must have removed it, for he could now see that the charges were strictly religious in nature. He had suspected that from the start.

We know that the Romans were commonly superstitious, and Pilate had several experiences on that day that could have shaken him severely. In the midst of the questioning of Christ, Pilate's wife had sent a message, warning him not to have anything to do with the innocent man, Jesus, because she had been warned about Him in a dream (Matthew 27:10). Further, Pilate may have been rattled by the utter calm that Jesus displayed. To risk Caesar's displeasure was bad enough, but if he offended the gods—what would happen then?

Jesus calmly responded to Pilate's many questions and then declared that the Jewish religious leaders had the greater guilt. By implication, He was saying that Pilate, the judge, had the lesser guilt. How totally uncommon for the prisoner to declare who was guilty and how much. As Pilate began to crumble under the pressure, Jesus continued to demonstrate His calm reliance on the guiding hand of the Father.

At the height of Pilate's desire to free Jesus, the Jews moved in on his political weakness. They shouted, "If you let this man go, you are no *friend of Caesar.*" To be a "friend of Caesar" meant that a man was loyal to the Emperor and was part of the ruling aristocracy. In effect, the Jews were saying that for Pilate to release Jesus would demonstrate disloyalty to Tiberius. The hidden threat was that if Pilate didn't go along with their desire to crucify Christ, they would make enough trouble to have Pilate removed from office. John makes it clear that when Pilate "heard" *those words* his resistance finally broke (John 19:13). In John's gospel, the Greek word for "hearing" always means to hear with comprehension; the words sank in and had their intended effect. Pilate knew what they were threatening.

PILATE SURRENDERS TO THE MOB

It was the day of Preparation of Passover Week, about the sixth hour.

"Here is your king," Pilate said to the Jews.

But they shouted, "Take him away! Take him away! Crucify him!"

"Shall I crucify your king?" Pilate asked.

"We have no king but Caesar," the chief priests answered.

Finally Pilate handed him over to them to be crucified. (John 19:14-16)

I find it quite significant that Pilate resisted the pressures brought on him throughout the morning and did not break until noon ("the sixth hour"). To understand the significance of that hour, we will need some background. Hoehner presents evidence that the Galileans (including Jesus and his followers) observed Passover on Thursday, whereas the Judeans (and the Temple officials) conducted Passover on Friday.[3] That explains how Jesus could share the Passover meal with his own disciples on one day and be slain as God's appointed Passover sacrifice on the following day. There were two different observances of Passover on consecutive days.

The Passover celebration looked back to that time when the death angel had passed over every Jewish home marked with the blood of a lamb (see Exodus 12). Any home in Egypt not marked on that night suffered death of a firstborn son. It was customary to begin slaying the Passover lambs at noon *(the sixth hour)* on Friday according to the custom of the Judeans. So at that very hour God's Lamb was surrendered to the religious leaders who put Him to death.

Pilate made a last weak attempt to sway the crowd, but when he failed he washed his hands before them, symbolically cleansing himself of any responsibility for what was to occur. An uproar was starting, and he had to avoid that at all costs (Matthew 27:24). Pilate had finally buckled under the stress brought upon him.

MEETING PRESSURE HEAD ON

I would like to offer a few suggestions about how you can face pressures that are put upon you.

1. How easy it is for the end to justify the means. To do what is expedient rather than what is right eventually leads to disaster. Here are some critical questions to guide you when you have to make decisions under pressure:

- As you consider God's standards, would this action be right—for you, for your family, for others?

[3]Ibid., 86-88.

- In a week or a year from now, will you feel good about your decision?
- Are you simply taking the easy way out?
- Are you merely forcing the answer to come out the way you want it, or are you being objective?

2. Many forces in life can put us under extreme pressure. How can we cope with it?

- Pray for the Lord to strengthen you to resist pressure.
- Get support and wisdom from other mature believers.
- Be willing to trust God, even if obeying Him leads to unjust suffering (see Philippians 2:8; Hebrews 5:8; 1 Peter 4:12-29).

A FINAL WORD

Every hour of the day a military aide stays within a few feet of the President of the United States. He carries a briefcase known as "The Football," which carries the orders that the President would give to unleash nuclear war upon the world. Imagine what it would be like to live with the stress of knowing that *you* might someday have to make such a decision. No wonder our Presidents seem to age excessively during their years in office.

Few Americans will ever have to worry about stress from "The Football," but each of us will face things at various points in our lives that *feel* just that intense. Only by relying on the Lord, His power, and His principles for life can we hope to bear up under the strain and do what is pleasing to Him. Jesus called upon those same resources during His stress test. That's a lead we can follow with confidence.

12

An X-Ray of Reality

I don't like feeling foolish any more than you do. But sometimes I get caught by a deficient set of facts. To give you an idea of what I'm talking about, let me tell you about what happened one August. At that time every year the drinking water where I live tastes bad because of algae growing in the warm lake waters. The water company dumps in great quantities of chlorine to kill the offending life-forms. That makes the water taste awful.

I decided to fix the taste problem by installing one of those water filters that you attach to the kitchen water faucet. It took only a few minutes to install the little metal cylinder that holds the filter, and I felt very pleased when I wrapped up the job. I decided to convince my family about the benefits of the new device by conducting a taste test of filtered and unfiltered water. My wife and children didn't know which glass had been filtered and which one had not, but they all picked the water that had passed through the filter as tasting the best. Needless to say, I was feeling pretty smug by that point.

In about three months I decided it was time to change the used filter and put in a new one. I carefully unscrewed the filter container and found—nothing! There was no used filter inside. There never had been! What about the taste test, you ask? There is only one chance in eight that my family would all pick the supposedly filtered water as tasting best when in reality it was no different at all. But they did. My original wrong assumption about the filter had been confirmed by a statistical fluke.

You see, reality isn't always what we think it should be. Fortunately, it didn't matter very much that I entrusted the water quality of our home to a nonexistent water filter. But each of us regularly relies on things that have far more import. We trust a life-partner, a career, or a way of raising children. But if we entrust ourselves to something that will ultimately fail us, then we are in trouble.

Christians, who have access to the inerrant Scriptures, have a tremendous advantage over others, in terms of knowing true reality. For example, one such reality is that a person must entrust himself to Jesus Christ to have eternal life. In addition, God has also revealed many principles for living that guide us in making the complex choices of modern life. He tells us in general terms what will work out for the best and what will not. But, in the short run, events may seem to contradict what God has said and may make the faith response look foolish.

A SHORT-SIGHTED VIEW OF REALITY

> Two other men, both criminals, were also led out with him to be executed. When they came to the place called The Skull, there they crucified him, along with the criminals—one on his right, the other on his left. Jesus said, "Father, forgive them, for they do not know what they are doing." And they divided up his clothes by casting lots.
>
> The people stood watching, and the rulers even sneered at him. They said, "He saved others; let him save himself if he is the Christ of God, the Chosen One."
>
> The soldiers also came up and mocked him. They offered him wine vinegar and said, "If you are the king of the Jews, save yourself."
>
> There was a written notice above him, which read:
> THIS IS THE KING OF THE JEWS.
>
> One of the criminals who hung there hurled insults at him: "Aren't you the Christ? Save yourself and us!" (Luke 23:32-39)

All those who watched as Christ was crucified encountered a reality that was very hostile to any kind of faith in Him. The hearts of many believers must have sunk to a nadir as they saw that the One to whom they had entrusted themselves now seemed powerless to resist Roman justice. The unbelievers who were watching had ample evidence to confirm their rejection of Jesus as the Messiah. Everything they saw seemed to cry out that His messianic claims were false. But behind such dark external "reality," the hand of God moved those events toward final victory. Only by using the expanded reality of revealed truth could those grim events be seen to move toward that glorious goal. The eye of faith must be able to look beyond the circumstances of the moment.

The night before, Jesus had warned His apostles about what was to follow by quoting the Isaiah prophecy that He would be "numbered among the transgressors." Now it was all taking place right before their eyes as He hung on a cross between two criminals.

Crucifixion inflicted tremendous suffering on its victims. Death came partly through starvation, partly through blood loss, and to some extent by exposure and long-term pain. The Romans found crucifixion so repulsive that Roman law prohibited its citizens from being crucified. The Roman statesman Cicero once said, "Even the mere word, cross, must remain far not only from the lips of the citizens of Rome, but also from their thoughts, their eyes, their ears." In spite of their revulsion against this penalty, the Romans had no hesitation in using it against foreigners such as Jesus.

I find it significant that Luke did not dwell on the unpleasantness of crucifixion. In fact, none of the gospel writers stressed that (though preachers often do). Instead, Luke focused on the *response* of those watching Christ's crucifixion. He paid careful attention to the varied reactions of the onlookers to the reality in front of them. I feel confident that this was Luke's intent because of the way he arranged his material. He presented four responses of condemnation toward Jesus and followed with four responses to vindicate Jesus.

The four condemning responses are expressed in verses 35-39. Here Luke described the people, the rulers, the soldiers, and one of the criminals. In his entire account Luke tended to downplay the role of the people, but here he grouped them with those antagonistic to Jesus. The other gospel writers also informed us that the people were mocking Jesus as the crucifixion took place (Matthew 27:39).

The Greek verb tense informs us that the rulers "sneered" at Jesus over a considerable period of time. I think it is likely that

Jesus hung on the cross beginning at nine o'clock in the morning and that the rulers responded to Him in this way until noon, when darkness fell on the land. As the rulers mocked Jesus, they quoted a psalm from the Old Testament, twisting it to suit their interpretation of the events at hand. We have seen the same tactic used on Jesus before. Satan tried the same thing as he tempted Jesus in the wilderness (see chapter 4). At the end of his description of these temptations, Luke stated that Satan would return at an opportune time (Luke 4:13). This was it. Satan did not speak with his own voice, but through the mouths of others as they jeered at the dying Messiah. The rulers derisively challenged Jesus to save Himself if He was who He had claimed to be.

The Roman soldiers also joined in the black humor of that occasion. The Jewish people hated the Roman army of occupation, and the feeling was mutual. These Romans felt little sympathy for this Jew dying on the cross. Over Jesus' head there hung a notice that read, "This is the King of the Jews." Roman justice demanded that the condemned person's crime be specified on the notice. What then was the crime? Can you find it? Well, Pilate couldn't find it either, and in writing those words on the notice he again made the point to the Jews that Jesus was innocent.

Roman society had a strong sense of class consciousness. The common soldiers of the execution squad could afford only the very cheapest kind of wine. It bordered on vinegar, a drink that would hardly be offered to a king. So in extending this drink to Jesus, they mocked Him in yet another way. They also took up the refrain of the others: "Save yourself."

Even one of the thieves hanging by Jesus joined the taunting crowd and rulers. Perhaps he hoped to ingratiate himself to the crowd, the Romans, and the religious leaders. Perhaps in that way he hoped he might be spared from death. After all, one other criminal, Barabbas, had already been delivered by the voice of the multitude from Roman justice that day. The thief's only source of hope seemed to be the surrounding crowd. By entrusting his hope to them, however, he unfortunately assured not only his physical death but his spiritual death as well. Such tragic consequences overtake those who do not take advantage of God's revelation in guiding their trust.

The people, the rulers, the soldiers, and the unfortunate thief all shared a common view of reality. They did not accept Jesus for who He really was, and they considered His death on the cross as the final proof of the correctness of their views. So that we do not condemn them too quickly, we should consider how common it is in our own culture to focus on short-term results.

LOOKING BEYOND THE CROSS

> But the other criminal rebuked him. "Don't you fear God," he said, "since you are under the same sentence? We are punished justly, for we are getting what our deeds deserve. But this man has done nothing wrong."
> Then he said, "Jesus, remember me when you come into your kingdom."
> Jesus answered him, "I tell you the truth, today you will be with me in paradise." (Luke 23:40-43)

Having considered those who condemned Christ, at this point in his account Luke shifts attention to those who spoke to vindicate Him. Those groups stand in stark contrast to one another, and the contrast begins with the two criminals. Consider carefully that the second criminal looked out on exactly the same scene as the first one. He saw the jeering mob, and beside him the Man from Nazareth, dying just as he was. But he obviously brought far more than just those few surrounding facts to guide his understanding of the whole situation.

The Greek verb tenses suggest that as frequently as the first thief mocked Jesus, this second one spoke up to defend Him. By doing so he made it clear that he did not share the earthbound perspective of the first thief. Instead, his view of "reality" had been expanded by the truth of God, so he responded to it in an entirely different way. The thief who defended Christ repeatedly called on the other thief to consider his own plight before God. He had only a few short hours to make whatever peace with God that he could. For him to waste his time by condemning an innocent man was the height of foolishness. That whole discussion may have been repeated several times in the course of the hours.

As death for all neared, the second thief said to Jesus, "Remember me when you come into your kingdom." To "remember" someone in the Jewish sense of that phrase does not mean to recall certain events in which they took part. That's how we might use such a phrase, but they used it differently. It means to remember others for good; to remember them in such a way

that you act in their behalf. This man was clearly looking beyond the moment at hand, when Jesus was hanging on the cross
dying. He was looking toward a time when Jesus would be in a
position to confer such benefits. He asserted that Jesus *would*
have a kingdom and implied that He was the King of the Jews,
as the notice over His head declared.

Jesus quickly rewarded such faith that could look beyond the
immediate circumstances. Jesus remembered the man for good
by bringing him to paradise that very day. By using the word
"paradise" the translators don't do the reader any favors, for
that word simply spells out in English the Greek word used by
Luke. To the Jewish mind the word represented the conditions
of the garden of Eden. The Jews imagined that when the Messiah set up His kingdom, He would refashion the world to resemble the Garden of Eden. There would be immediate com-
munion with God, an absence of the effect of sin, and tremendous bounty on every hand.

The contrast between the two thieves reminds me of a verse
Luke recorded earlier in his gospel. Jesus had said, "Whoever
wants to save his life will lose it, but whoever loses his life for
Me will save it" (Luke 9:24). The first thief had tried to save his
own life and had lost it. The second thief, who defended Christ,
would lose his life for Jesus' sake and save it. The two thieves
who hung on either side of Jesus illustrated quite clearly the
great difference it makes to have faith to guide one's choices in
the face of contrary "reality."

FURTHER VINDICATION

> It was now about the sixth hour, and darkness came over the
> whole land until the ninth hour, for the sun stopped shining. And
> the curtain of the temple was torn in two. Jesus called out with a
> loud voice, "Father, into your hands I commit my spirit." When he
> had said this, he breathed his last.
>
> The centurion, seeing what had happened, praised God and
> said, "Surely this was a righteous man." When all the people who
> had gathered to witness this sight saw what took place, they beat
> their breasts and went away. But all those who knew him, includ-
> ing the women who had followed him from Galilee, stood at a
> distance, watching these things. (Luke 23:44-49)

The second person who spoke in defense of Christ did so
without words, but with a message of compelling power. God

the Father spoke through supernatural events first in the heavens and then within the Temple itself. Starting at noon when the sun reached its zenith, darkness fell over the whole land until three in the afternoon. Some think that that darkness extended over the whole world, while others believe that it covered only the city of Jerusalem. I don't like either of those views and prefer the idea that the darkness extended over the entire land of Israel. In this way, the Father spoke eloquently to authenticate the claims of the One who hung on the cross.

Some have suggested that the darkness was caused by a solar eclipse, but they simply misunderstand astronomy. It was the time of Passover, which occurs during the full moon. When the moon is full, it stands in exactly the opposite side of the sky as the sun. So it would have been physically impossible for the moon to block the light of the sun, as it does in a solar eclipse. No, this darkness had a totally supernatural origin. I think the darkness that God sent was identical to that which He sent in the time of the Exodus (Exodus 14:20), a gloom so deep as never to be forgotten by those who experienced it. Thus, God spoke in cosmic terms to the entire nation.

The second sign God gave occurred before the eyes of a very few. He caused the curtain in the Temple to split down the middle. I don't know what the curtains in your house are like, but if I wanted to I could tear the ones in my house in half. The curtain in the Temple, however, was sixty feet wide and thirty feet high and had a thickness equal to the *width* of a man's palm. It took over three hundred priests to hoist the curtain into place, and it was replaced every three years so that deterioration of the fabric would not occur. The curtain stood between the Holy Place and the Holy of Holies. It was no human hand that ripped this curtain in two. Among its other meanings, the ripping of the curtain probably communicated that the way between man and God had now been opened through the death of God's own Messiah. When it first occurred, I'm sure only a few of the priests even knew about the event. But such a thing cannot long be hidden, and perhaps that helps to explain how a number of the priests trusted in Christ during the early days of the church. (Acts 6:7). So it was that in cosmic signs to the people and in supernatural miracles before the priesthood, God the Father spoke to vindicate the Son.

Finally Luke brings forward the final two witnesses to speak for Jesus by their responses to the overall situation. The first is

the Roman centurion who led the execution party. After watching Jesus die, he repeatedly praised God and declared the innocence of Christ. What this man had seen transformed his whole
opinion. We can only imagine what it must have taken to overcome his dislike for the Jewish people and his revulsion against
anyone who was being crucified.

The people who began by condemning Christ also changed
their attitudes because of the events that took place. Many of
them "beat their breasts," symbolizing their remorse over what
had happened. Luke used the very same word (Luke 18:13)
when he described the repentant tax collector who was so
ashamed of his sins that he could not even look up to heaven.
Those people came to jeer, but having seen everything, their
hearts had turned. Perhaps that explains why in a few short
weeks so many thousands of people in Jerusalem trusted in
Jesus as their Messiah when Peter preached on the day of Pente-
cost.

A BACKWARD GLANCE

All of the people involved in this story were looking at the
same set of external events. Jesus, in whom so many had placed
great hope, seemed powerless to prevent His own death on the
cross. Those who did not have a spiritual perspective could see
only the external realities, and so they joined in condemnation
of Jesus.

However, another group of people who believed in Him responded very differently because they had additional revelation
to help them interpret the situation. Through faith they could
take a longer view and look beyond the realities of that moment.

Chart 9	
CONDEMNATION	**VINDICATION**
1 People	5 Second thief
2 Rulers	6 God
3 Soldiers	7 Centurion
4 First thief	8 People

All history is selective, and Luke arranged his account of the crucifixion to contrast the responses of the people who saw it. This can be best seen by looking at chart 9.

Perhaps by this arrangement Luke was implying that the people in the first column should have listened to the testimony of their counterparts in the second column and responded to Jesus in faith. For example, the first thief should have considered the remorse and repentance of the multitude after they had seen all, and he himself should have repented of his sins.

RESPONDING TO THE REALITY OF THE CROSS

Use the following applicational ideas to sharpen your own understanding of what faith is and how you respond to short-term situations.

1. I find that believers don't usually understand what biblical faith is. Sometimes that's because they have been soured on faith through exposure to some distortion of the real thing.

- Faith is *not* some inner experience or intuition totally separate from our ability to reason. That's mysticism. We have a faith that *can* be explained, is based on revelation, and involves the shared experience of other believers. Faith does not involve some secret insight that is magically given to one person.

- Faith is *not* some emotion, mood, or experience. That's emotionalism. I don't think the second thief (hanging on a cross) felt very good, but he had a lot of faith!

- Faith is *not* knowledge alone (even biblical knowledge). That's intellectualism or Pharisaism. I hope it's obvious by this time that I am firmly supportive of biblical knowledge; it is absolutely essential to our salvation and godly behavior. But biblical knowledge is not faith, even though it provides a basis for faith.

Now I would like to define what biblical faith *is*. Faith is a response to reality, including unseen reality. *Faith is a response of surrender or obedience to the reality of revealed truth*. In salvation, the emphasis falls on the surrender aspect, as a person surrenders himself to Jesus Christ as his Savior. In Christian living the emphasis lies on obedience to the teachings of the Lord.

To help clarify what faith is, consider the following chart:

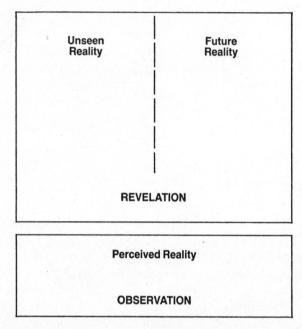

Those who don't know Jesus Christ can only respond to the reality that they can see, perceived reality. Like those who condemned Jesus, their observable world imprisons them. But believers have access to a far larger perspective of reality, including unseen and future reality, both revealed through the Word of God.

The Holy Spirit would be one example of an unseen reality of which the Scriptures inform us. Jesus held out a future reality to the second thief when he promised him that He would accompany him in paradise that very day. That man could not have known that, apart from Jesus' telling him. But it was a fact. It was a reality.

I would like for you to respond to the following statements:
- The world doesn't live by faith, and I have/have not conformed to such a viewpoint.
- I have/have not reacted against faulty forms of faith and denied true forms of faith much room in my life.

With my background as an engineer, I like to consider myself a no-nonsense kind of person. People like me may be more prone than most to let distortions of real faith turn us off. At some point we may have been exposed to mysticism, emotionalism, or intellectualism and reacted by saying within ourselves,

"If that's what living by faith is all about, then you can keep it."
If you have overreacted to some situation like that, I would like
to encourage you to reconsider the whole issue and give faith a
larger place in your life.

2. Americans are constantly encouraged to look for short-term
results or payoff. As a culture we have embraced pragmatism;
we determine what is true by looking at short-term, positive,
measurable results. But many of the results and rewards of
living for Christ lie beyond our view or measure. That puts our
faith in tension.

- Have you given up on living by faith because you did not
  see immediate results and rewards?

3. Biblical faith always involves real-life responses to God and
His Word. Perhaps you know of a response you personally need
to make in faith. Why not commit yourself to do it now?

- The area I need to respond in
- The specific thing I need to do

A FINAL WORD

All of us have to respond to life situations in one way or
another. By our behavior, we will entrust our lives to something—a person, a concept, a truth that we hold as reality. But
biblical faith always involves more than mental assent to an
idea. It always involves action.

In the last century, a young man destined to be the ruler of
Germany sat in a chemistry class, learning about the Leidenfrost effect. If you have ever ironed a shirt, then you may know
what this effect is. Perhaps you have licked your finger before
touching an iron to find out if it was hot. When you touched the
hot iron, your finger didn't get burned because of the Leidenfrost effect. The moisture flashes to steam and forms a small
vapor barrier between the sensitive finger and the hot surface
of the iron. Now let me inform you of one other physical fact;
lead melts at a temperature above 500 degrees Farenheit.

After teaching the whole class about the Leidenfrost effect,
the chemistry teacher approached the young man destined to
rule. He asked whether the young man believed in the principles of chemistry. When the boy said yes, the teacher asked him
to go over to a bowl and soak his hands in ammonia. Then he
had the boy cup his hands together. Into the young man's out-

stretched hands the teacher poured molten lead! Because the ammonia formed a vapor barrier (the Leidenfrost effect), his hands were not burned.

Believing in the Leidenfrost effect was *not* faith, but trusting his hands to it was!

In a similar way, God wants us to respond with living faith to the realities that He sets before us.

13
Not in Vain

In the lush, misty hills of Vietnam lies the A Shau valley. In this picture postcard setting rises a hill with a harsh American name—Hamburger Hill. A name well earned.

For ten brutal days, American paratroopers had assaulted the North Vietnamese who were entrenched atop Hamburger Hill. For nine straight days the battle-hardened enemy beat back the American attack. Finally, on the tenth bloody day, the assault forces drove the enemy off the summit. To win that height, 430 American soldiers had given their lives, and many who stood on that summit thought of friends suddenly ripped from this world.

Within hours after the hard-won victory, orders arrived from headquarters, directing that the hill be abandoned because the position was considered strategically worthless. Someone had decided that it wasn't needed. The paratroopers greeted those orders with cold fury; for the first time in American military history, the troops almost mutinied.

This tragic story demonstrates that each of us wants to live for something; we don't want to live or die in vain. Whether knowingly or not, every man searches for meaning and purpose to his life.

It may strike you as a mystery that Paul connects meaning and purpose for our lives with the resurrection of Christ, but that's exactly what he does in 1 Corinthians 15. Paul tells us that, because of Christ's victory over sin and death at the cross, you and I can live for Him in full knowledge that we do not live in vain. As we put our faith in Jesus Christ and then live for Him in a way that is pleasing to God, we are making an eternal investment that we will never regret.

Such meaning and purpose in Christ will prove vital at several crucial points in our earthly life. Research reveals that at about ages thirty, forty, and fifty, men look back over their years and take stock of their lives. An evaluation that looms even larger comes sometime after age sixty, when virtually every man evaluates his life and judges whether it has been worthwhile or wasted. If his backward glance reveals drifting purpose and faded value, then his latter years may be spent in bitterness and regret. But a life of purpose, meaning, and lasting value can give a sense of closure that allows a person to face the last years with a satisfied feeling inside. How true that should be of believers.

JESUS AMONG THE DEAD

> Now there was a man named Joseph, a member of the Council, a good and upright man, who had not consented to their decision and action. He came from the Judean town of Arimathea and he was waiting for the kingdom of God. Going to Pilate, he asked for Jesus' body. Then he took it down, wrapped it in linen cloth and placed it in a tomb cut in the rock, one in which no one had yet been laid. It was Preparation Day, and the Sabbath was about to begin. (Luke 23:50-54)

In Joseph of Arimathea we find a godly man, "waiting for the kingdom of God." Surprisingly, we find that he held membership in the Sanhedrin, the ruling council comprised chiefly of Sadducees and teachers of the law. The Sanhedrin had orchestrated Jesus' death, so it is doubly surprising that one of its members approached Pilate to ask for His body. The explanation lies in the fact that Joseph had become a disciple of Jesus (Matthew 27:57).

I want to concentrate for a moment on the fact that Jesus was truly *dead*. That may seem strange, but some have tried to write off the resurrection by claiming that Jesus was not really dead at the time.[1] But to say that, one must deny the statements of the

[1]For an example of this, see Hugh J. Schonfield, *The Passover Plot* (New York: Bantam, 1971).

biblical record. The Sanhedrin wanted Jesus, who had caused them no end of trouble, dead. They spared no pains in accomplishing that goal. They had stood among the crowd around the cross to confirm that their efforts had been crowned with success. You can be sure that no member of the council went home that day before satisfying himself that Jesus was dead.

Consider too the Romans. Once Pilate had given the death sentence, Jesus was taken by *Roman* troops out to the cross to be executed. The Romans had executed thousands of Jews in this manner and knew how to do the job. So the Sanhedrin watched while experts carried out their will. The Roman centurion declined to break Christ's legs to hasten His death, after confirming with a spear point that He had already died. When Pilate received Joseph's request to bury Jesus, he did not grant it until he had personally asked the centurion in charge to confirm that Jesus was dead (Mark 15:44). Only then did he give the body to Joseph. We can be sure that the body Joseph took down from the cross had no vestige of life in it.

A SHORT TOUR OF THE TOMB

Try to use your imagination for a moment to picture the tomb in which Jesus was buried. Being a man of wealth, Joseph placed Jesus in his own freshly-made tomb cut from rock (Matthew 27:57-60). The tomb probably had a round door leading to an antechamber about ten feet square. In this area the mourners made final preparation of the body. The walls around the room usually contained shelves cut from the rock; these shelves were used to hold each of the bodies placed in the tomb. In this way, whole familes could be buried together, much as is our own custom. The door of the tomb consisted of a large round stone, rolled in a stone groove to control access to the doorway. These closure stones weighed many tons and were often accompanied by a smaller stone, rolled up to one side to prevent the large stone from moving.

Joseph probably put Jesus in his own tomb not only out of personal kindness, but also because he was sorely pressed for time. Jesus died about three o'clock in the afternoon, and very little time remained before the sun would set and the Sabbath would begin. Because no work could be done after sunset, Joseph had to move quickly to obtain Pilate's permission to take Christ's body down from the cross and to place it in his tomb. In all probability, Joseph did not finish the preparations of the body that he had hoped to accomplish. That would explain what happened next.

VIGIL OF SORROW

> The women who had come with Jesus from Galilee followed Joseph and saw the tomb and how his body was laid in it. Then they went home and prepared spices and perfumes. But they rested on the Sabbath in obedience to the commandment. (Luke 23:55-56)

These loyal women had been with Jesus for a long time, and they didn't leave His body until they had seen exactly where Joseph had put it. Some skeptics have claimed that the tomb was later empty because the women found the wrong tomb. But the women knew exactly where to look.

Besides the women, Joseph was assisted in his work by Nicodemus (John 20:39). At least two members of the Sanhedrin had trusted in Christ and were honoring Him in His death.

JESUS AMONG THE LIVING

> On the first day of the week, very early in the morning, the women took the spices they had prepared and went to the tomb. They found the stone rolled away from the tomb, but when they entered, they did not find the body of the Lord Jesus. (Luke 24:1-3)

The word *sabbath* comes from a Hebrew word that means seventh. The seventh day was Saturday. Jesus was crucified on Friday, the sixth day of the week, and the women did not return to the tomb until the first day of the following week, which was Sunday in our terminology. As God-fearing people, they did not work or journey on the sabbath day, Saturday.

Jesus had said that he would rise on "the third day," and He stayed in the tomb for parts of three different days. His body was placed in the tomb on Friday, the first day, and was unobserved in the tomb on Saturday, the second day. He departed from the tomb alive on Sunday, the third day.

As the women were walking on their way to the tomb, they expected that the stone would present a big problem (Mark 16:3). They didn't know it, but God had removed an even bigger problem than that from the scene. On Saturday, the religious leaders had obtained Pilate's permission to post an armed guard at the tomb. They remembered what Jesus had said about rising on the third day, and they wanted to prevent any theft of the body that might be used to spread such a lie (Matthew 27:62-66). With Pilate's permission, they posted a guard and then placed a seal, probably on the boundary surface between the large stone covering the door and the small stone beside it. The seal meant that the tomb was not to be opened without Pilate's permission.

But God had the nerve to open Christ's tomb without permission! While the women were still approaching the tomb, an angel of the Lord had arrived and thrown the stone aside. He also frightened the guards to the point that they first collapsed in fright and later ran away to report to the chief priests (Matthew 28:2-15).

Those guards would only have run away from mortal danger, because a Roman guard could be executed for abandoning his post. The religious leaders not only paid them to spread an erroneous story, but also promised them that they would keep Pilate from punishing them. Luke tells us only that when the women arrived, they found that the stone had been rolled away and the body of Jesus was gone. He does not mention the guards, because they had already fled.

An empty tomb in itself doesn't mean a whole lot; that could exist for any number of reasons. The town in which you live probably has some empty tombs. The reason *this* empty tomb is so important is that *God has revealed to us why it was empty.* God spoke first through angelic messengers and later through His risen Son, appearing alive before His followers. The empty tomb means little, but the living Savior means everything.

A FORWARDING ADDRESS

> While they were wondering about this, suddenly two men in clothes that gleamed like lightning stood beside them. In their fright the women bowed down with their faces to the ground, but the men said to them, "Why do you look for the living among the dead? He is not here; he has risen! Remember how he told you, while he was still with you in Galilee: 'The Son of Man must be delivered into the hands of sinful men, be crucified and on the third day be raised again.'" Then they remembered his words. (Luke 24:4-8)

After His death, fear and despair overwhelmed most of

Christ's disciples. Only a few, like the women and the two Sanhedrin members, dared to move in public. Most of Christ's
disciples hid themselves, trembling at the possibility that the
authorities might arrive and haul them off at any moment. They
were looking back at those last few years and thinking that it
had all been in vain. They thought they had found the Messiah,
but He had been taken away from them, and they were left only
with regret.

In every description of the disciples, both male and female,
we find that they were very slow to accept what had really
happened. Christ's death so shattered them that they struggled
to begin accepting that He had truly risen from the grave. Using
the remainder of Luke's account, let's consider for a moment
how they gradually changed from despair to confusion, to
shock at His appearing, and finally to triumphant joy.

AN AMAZING TRANSFORMATION

Two of the first disciples Jesus encountered were making a
journey to Emmaus. Jesus supernaturally prevented them from
grasping who He was as He probed them on the events of the
previous days. Then He rebuked them for being "slow of heart"
to believe all that had been told to them beforehand (Luke
24:25). The women had fled straight from the tomb to the men
to tell them what had happened, but the men had responded
with unbelief and scorn.

Later in the day, after Jesus had appeared to Peter and James
as well as others, all the disciples had gathered and were still
having a hard time believing what they had seen. That's when
Thomas made his memorable statement that he would not believe that Jesus had risen unless he could see the nail marks in
His hands and put his fingers there (John 20:25). At that very
moment Jesus appeared in their midst and called on Thomas to
"stop doubting and believe" (John 21:27). Only then did they all
accept what had occurred. Jesus had indeed risen from the
dead.

Luke ended his account of Christ's life by describing how the
disciples worshiped Jesus and then returned to Jerusalem with
great joy (Luke 24:52). In his sequel (Acts 1-8), Luke described
how those who had hidden in fear of death went out with
tremendous boldness to witness all over Jerusalem, and elsewhere, too. An incredible reversal took place in their attitudes
and behavior because they had been with their risen Lord.

THE RESURRECTION OF JESUS—A FACT!

I want to present what I see as the leading reasons that the resurrection of Christ must have happened exactly the way the Scriptures tell it.

First of all, Christ's opponents could never produce His body to refute the claims of His followers. You can imagine how quickly this popular movement would have dissipated, if they had only brought His dead body before the crowds. You can also be sure that the Sanhedrin that plotted so carefully to put Him to death searched far and wide to try to produce His body. They thought they had solved their problems when they put Him to death, but He didn't stay where they put Him. The leaders could not just produce another body, because Jesus had been seen by too many people, and His appearance was well-known. Thousand of Jewish worshipers came to Jerusalem from around the Mediterranean world to worship at Passover, and many of them had observed Jesus firsthand.

Second, whenever you see a big effect, you should look back earlier to find a big cause. Only big causes produce big effects. Let me explain. The explosive spread of Christianity within the hostile environment of Judaism and Roman persecution is what I would call a big effect. Christianity first arose in a Jewish setting that found it absolutely abhorrent. The Romans did not hinder Christianity much in the early days, but they did later when it became apparent that the Christians would not worship the Roman pantheon of deities. That was considered treason in the eyes of many Romans. I submit that for most of the Roman world to become Christian within two centuries after Christ's death constitutes a big effect. Can you really get such a big effect from someone lying dead in a tomb? I say no. To get such a big effect requires a cause as big as the resurrection of Jesus from the dead.

The resurrection filled Jesus' disciples with explosive zeal because they knew that even if they lost their lives, they had not lived in vain. They had something to live and die for.

Third, Paul and James, the Lord's brother, would never have trusted Jesus as their Messiah apart from His appearing to them after the resurrection. Only an encounter with the resurrected Lord could change Paul from a murderous persecutor of Christ's disciples into an equally zealous proponent of Jesus as the Messiah (Acts 9). The same is true for James (see John 7:5 about the unbelief of Jesus' brothers).

The apostles and others were willing to die for their faith because they knew that the resurrection was true. Liberal scholars have claimed that the apostles fabricated Christ's resurrection simply because the church wanted to believe that it had happened. But such views run into fatal psychological difficulty when we realize that these men had to lay their lives on the line for what they were saying. People simply will not die for a lie.

If the apostles had conspired to fabricate a resurrection lie, they would have produced a more airtight story. They would not have written four gospels that tend to stress different aspects of the event from different viewpoints. To sell a lie, it would have been far easier to fabricate one simple story and get everybody to tell that. But the apostles didn't worry about that. They were telling the truth. They knew their story hung together; they had been there to see it. Further, a fabricated story would never have included women as witnesses, because Jewish society did not accept their testimony about anything. Finally, a fabricated story would have contained no evidence of residual unbelief (Matthew 28:17). But *God* need not feel insecure, because few people don't believe. He could afford to tell the truth and not worry about unbelief.

THE DOMINO EFFECT

Even some believers hesitate to accept the resurrection because it does not fit well in a modern world that feels skepticism toward the supernatural. But the fact of the matter is that the resurrection links up with other things that Christians desperately want to believe. Paul connects the reality of eternal life with the reality of Christ's physical resurrection (Colossians 2:13). If Jesus didn't rise from the dead, then there is no such thing as eternal life. That's a loss few Christians would be willing to accept.

Paul also links the resurrection of Christ to the power God has given us for Christian life (Romans 8:11). Without the resurrection, sin still reigns over our mortal bodies (Romans 6:12), and we remain dead in our sins (1 Corinthians 15:17).

I have given you only a few examples among many of the importance of the resurrection. These things are theologically connected to the resurrection by the writings of the New Testament. Like dominoes in a row, if the resurrection falls, then other things that Christians value dearly fall as well. Believers cannot reasonably choose to defend only those parts of the Scriptures that they find comfortable. The whole thing stands or falls together. I say it stands. More importantly, God says it stands.

THE RESURRECTION AND YOU

Use the following applicational ideas to drive home the truth of the resurrection in your own life.

1. The resurrection of Christ proves that God has accepted His sacrifice for our sins. The penalty for our sins has been paid in full.

- I agree that my entire guilt before God has been taken away.

2. The resurrection of Christ brings every believer a new power to live for God. The *dominating* power of sin has been broken. In Romans 6 and 8 we are told that believers share the same kind of power that raised Jesus from the dead. Only by our access to this power can we successfully resist the domination of our sinful nature. Peter tells us that God has "given us everything we need for life and godliness" (2 Peter 1:3). Through the presence of His Holy Spirit, God has given us all that we need to live our lives unto Him.

- I agree that God has granted me power through the Holy Spirit to live for Him.
- Are you taking advantage of this resource that God has provided, or has your behavior remained unchanged since you trusted Christ?

3. We can respond to Christ's resurrection with thankfulness that living for God is not a futile gesture. Managing our lives for Him will have eternal significance. Perhaps you will find it appropriate to express yourself in prayer thanking God right now.

A FINAL WORD

At the midpoint of the Civil War, a solemn journey brought Abraham Lincoln to the scene of the bloodiest battlefield, Gettysburg. Here, in a hard-fought battle, tens of thousands of Union soldiers were slain in the hills and fields near the town. Lincoln had come to dedicate a national cemetery to honor the Union dead. He gave the very short speech that we call the

Gettysburg Address. He looked back at the awesome loss of life and noted that these men had made the ultimate sacrifice that anyone could make. They had given their own lives for a cause that they believed in. But when they perished, they did not know whether or not they had died in vain. Lincoln said that only by winning the final victory could the Union make those men's profound sacrifice worthwhile. He challenged all present with the responsibility to win the war so that their dead companions would not have died for nothing. Two more bloody years of doubt passed before that question was finally answered.

No one who believes in Jesus Christ will ever have to face such doubt. The message Jesus brings us differs radically from the one that Lincoln gave to his audience. Jesus tells us that the final victory has *already been won*. He settled that first by dying for our sins and then rising from the dead. As we continue our struggle, our fight in life, we can do so without ever worrying that it will prove a waste.

With Paul, I reach this conclusion: "Therefore my dear brothers, stand firm. Let nothing move you. Always give yourselves fully to the work of the Lord, because you know that *your labor in the Lord is not in vain*" (1 Corinthians 15:58, italics added).

Moody Press, a ministry of the Moody Bible Institute, is designed for education, evangelization, and edification. If we may assist you in knowing more about Christ and the Christian life, please write us without obligation: Moody Press, c/o MLM, Chicago, Illinois 60610